You Can Never Have Too Much

S.E.X.

(Self-Examination)

Stop Blaming Others & Take
Responsibility

❖

Laura A. Franklin

"You Can Never Have Too Much S.E.X" by Laura A. Franklin. ISBN 978-1-63868-205-9.

Published 2025 by Virtualbookworm.com Publishing, P.O. Box 9949, College Station, TX 77842, US.

CONTENTS

Acknowledgements

For my children, grandchildren, and godchildren: I hope y'all learn THE lesson before y'all learn YOUR lesson.

❖

It's hard being the first, but it's harder being the last. Make it count!!

❖

Thank you, Friend!

Caution: Y'all might not invite me back once you read this.

Foreword

As the author of this book, I want to make it clear that while I am a licensed driver, I am not a licensed therapist. The insights shared here come from my own experiences, heartfelt conversations with friends, lessons from family, wisdom from my community, and even encounters with perfect strangers. This book is not intended to diagnose or treat any conditions you may be facing. Instead, it serves as a spark—one that may stir memories of the past, inspire hope for the future, and encourage deep self-reflection. By the time you finish reading, you might feel compelled to apologize—to others, to yourself, to God... maybe even to me.

I know that at first glance, the title of this book might lead readers to believe it's solely about sex. In reality, only two sections are dedicated to intimacy in that sense. Growing up and striving to become the woman God intended me to be, I didn't truly understand what intimacy meant. My lack of knowledge in this area created challenges in every relationship where sex was merely an event rather than an experience. The way we approach **Self-EXamination** shapes how we move forward. It's never easy to look within and confront our own flaws—whether in the pursuit of self-improvement, personal growth, or simply becoming a better version of ourselves. But true transformation begins with honest reflection.

For a significant part of my life, I sought validation from others. More often than not, it was fleeting, superficial, or came at a cost I wasn't willing to pay. I landed my first job at 18, and in every workplace since, I've encountered someone—whether a colleague or a superior—who had an issue with me. Not necessarily because I was the problem, but simply because I existed in a space they didn't think I belonged. I remember being hired at a well-known organization, only to feel the weight of judgment the moment I walked through the doors. The stares, the eye rolls—it was clear they had already decided I wasn't fit for the role. They had heard I was coming, skimmed my résumé over their morning coffee, and written me off before I even had a chance to prove myself.

I do not take lightly the responsibilities I have—to God, to myself, to my family, my friends, and my community. With that said, I must be honest: my name is Laura, and I am on a Spectrum. But if we're being truly honest with ourselves, we can acknowledge that in some way, we all are. Maybe you find yourself tapping your leg when there's no music playing, blinking repeatedly, or twitching your nose. Perhaps you're obsessive about how things are arranged on a floor, wall, or table. You may have ADD or ADHD, struggle with focus, or get easily distracted (*SQUIRREL!*). Whatever it is, society often labels these behaviors as "irregular" or "not normal"—but the truth is, they're just part of the vast and varied spectrum of human experience.

From what I can recall, it all started in my teens. I found myself counting tiles—on the ceiling, on the floor—seeing intricate patterns that I assumed no one else noticed. As a passenger in a moving vehicle, my mind would fixate on patterns and shapes beyond just the clouds. I can't quite explain why, but it fascinated me. Do you remember those old classroom ceiling tiles with tiny holes in them? I sure do. I would count the holes and the tiles in sets of 10, 20, or 30, arranging them in my mind like pieces of a puzzle. I would create shapes and patterns, only later realizing they aligned with geometric principles. I even counted the slats on the floor—2 and 1, 2 and 1—until they formed a perfect, even sequence. And if they didn't? I would start over until they did.

I LOVE numbers. I have a near-photographic memory when it comes to them. As a child, I was a walking phone book—back when people relied on those thick white and yellow pages. But in my house, my mother didn't need one. She had me. I could recall addresses, phone numbers, license plates, Social Security numbers, driver's license numbers, VIN numbers on vehicles, and even strange sequences from computers with ease. Numbers just made sense to me in a way that words sometimes didn't. At the same time, I can become mentally overstimulated by clusters of lights mixed with bold colors, loud noises, or too much attention. I want to be noticed—but for the right reasons, not just for the sake of standing out.

I also have an uncanny ability to track dates. I'm a walking calendar—if you mention an upcoming event, I can usually tell you what day of the week it falls on without even thinking about it. My kids will understand now; there are sequences constantly running through my mind that I can't quite explain. But numbers aren't my only quirk. I've also struggled with reading comprehension since the 5th grade. If I don't read out loud, I won't retain what I've read. It's a challenge I still navigate today, but I've learned how to make it work for me. And don't even get me started on music.

Most musicians will tell you they constantly hear harmonies. That's me. I remember watching a live choir recording once, and when the final project was complete and published, it didn't sound the same. I know that production companies often go back to the studio afterward to layer in additional harmonies or fill in gaps for a more polished sound, and I believe this is what happened. But even before those edits, I could already hear the missing parts in my head. The challenge? My ears, brain, and mouth don't always communicate in sync, making it difficult to sing what I hear. For about two years, I had the opportunity to teach songs to a choir when we didn't have a pianist. I sang and taught all three vocal parts by ear. What I loved most about this experience was that the choir trusted me. They believed in my ability, and when they saw the results of their learning, it was deeply fulfilling. I loved every moment of it! This, too, is part of being on the spectrum.

When I was a kid, the term most commonly used was "Special Ed" or "SPED." Back then, calling someone a "SPED" was meant as an insult—a joke. That was until I truly understood what it meant... and realized I was one of them. I'll never forget when an educator mentioned a local school's SPED program, and it hit me in a way I didn't expect. It bothered me so much that I prayed and asked God for forgiveness for every time I had used that term in ignorance. It was a lesson I carry to this day: be careful what you tease others for—you may one day find yourself in their shoes. For those who often tell me to "slow down," now you understand why I move so fast. My mind is constantly racing, moving at a speed my legs can barely keep up with. I try, but the thoughts never stop. My pastor once said something profound about mothers: "When they lay down at night, their bodies rest, but their minds keep replaying what did and didn't happen that day, all while thinking ahead to tomorrow." Now, imagine that same mother, and she is on the spectrum.

The laundry is a never-ending task. There's always something out of place at home that catches my eye, prompting me to fix it. Disorder doesn't sit well with me. Yet, I find comfort in what I call organized chaos. I can embrace these quirks because they are an essential part of who I am and what drives me forward. And that's okay. I've accepted it. Eventually, you will too.

Introduction

If I could speak to my younger self, I would say:

"Speak up for yourself when that grown man touches you inappropriately, don't stay silent—fight for yourself." I would tell her that Ricky Jones is the real MVP of young boys. I would tell her to scream at the top of her lungs when that white man chases you down the street in College Park, GA. I would tell her to drown the boy who tried to pull off her bathing suit underwater. I would tell her to punch every boy in the throat who makes a crude comment about her body and her face. I would tell her to slap every boy who refused to believe she could launch a football across a field without hesitation, play both running back and receiver, and still march in the marching band. I would tell her you are powerful!

I would also tell her to "Bash your brother-in-law's head in for laying his hands on your pregnant sister—no matter how much she defends him, even when she sends you home for calling Madea and telling her the truth." I would tell her to shove Otis off his go-kart for calling you flat-chested and choosing her sister over her. I would tell her to wait for Horace—yes, he's a nerd, but he's worth it. That older guy, Michael, the one she thinks she wants? He only wants one thing. I'd warn her that Michael is 18 years old and still in the 9th grade. He's not smart, he's not your future, and he will only hold you back.

I would warn her that by the age of 16, you will give herself to a boy who will hurt you—physically and emotionally—because of his own narcissism and insecurities. And that experience will shape the way you see Black men for years to come. But most of all, I would tell her that *none of it is your fault*—even when your abusers try to make you believe it was.

I would assure her that none of it was your fault—you simply didn't know what real love was. I would tell her to "Brace yourself", because life will test you in ways you never imagined. You will battle breast cancer—not once, but twice—and you will survive. You will write books, stand on important stages, shake hands, kiss babies, and inspire countless people. But none of it will fill the void you have been unknowingly keeping open, waiting for true love to find its way in. The truth is, you won't truly understand what love is until you turn 55. I would also tell her that you will make history, becoming one of the first—if not *the* first—African American women to serve as a Housing Commissioner in your city. But no matter how hard you fight, no matter how much you prove yourself, they will never fully let you in. They will refuse to respect you, refuse to include you, refuse to acknowledge you—despite the title and despite the accomplishments. And yet, you will stand tall.

The last thing I would tell her is this: it's okay to be on a spectrum. It's what makes you unique. Embrace it. Yes, putting a spoon up to your ear lets you hear other people's conversations—and that's just one of the little quirks that make you *you*. Know that Jesus loves you more than any man ever could. He is the only one who can truly fill that void you've been carrying. None of the offenses against you were your fault, but for a while, it will feel like your burden—because you can be stubborn and strong-willed. One day, that burden will become your fuel, and it will drive you for the rest of your life.

Chapter One

S.E.X. Appeal – Who AM I?

At 12 years old, everything in my world started shifting. Puberty hit, and I discovered my "musical ear," I fully embraced my tomboy phase, and I fell in love with sports. I found my voice—both on and off the field—and learned to stand up for myself and others. Life felt like a whirlwind of exciting and defining moments.

Basketball, track and field, and flag football became my passions. On the basketball court, I played power forward. On the track team, I ran the 4x100 relay and took on the high jump. And in football, I played both quarterback and wide receiver. But despite my skills, I held myself back. In basketball, I was afraid of my own talent, hesitant to "perform" in front of a crowd. That fear kept me on the bench more than I'd like to admit. It was a scorching day in May in College Park, Georgia, and I was at a home game for my middle school's basketball team. As usual, I had a basketball and a football with me. Walking across the court before the game, I started spinning the basketball on one finger, completely unaware of who was watching. The girls' basketball coach called me over.

"What's your name? What grade are you in?" she asked.

After I answered, she hit me with a question that changed everything:

"You want to play on the team?"

I said yes. And just like that, I was in.

Since the season had already started, there was only one jersey number left: 56. *"A linebacker's number,* I thought." But it was mine now. When I got home, I couldn't wait to tell my mother and my oldest brother. My oldest brother had played basketball in high school, and I wanted nothing more than to follow in his footsteps. I was excited—but I wasn't prepared for how brutal practice would be. I only wanted to play for fun. My coach was dead serious.

One game, my mother and brother came to watch me play. Only... I didn't play. I sat on that bench the entire time, my excitement turned into quiet shame. The ride home was quiet except for the comments from my oldest brother. He teased me for not getting any game time—he had no idea I cried in the shower that night. Not because of what he said, but because I wanted so badly to make them proud.

Joining the Flag Football team was a different battle altogether. Girls weren't treated fairly. The boys were bullies—loud, obnoxious, and full of what I like to call "waterhead" energy. Waterhead boys are the ones who run their mouths, say dumb things just to get under your skin, or push you away before you can prove yourself. These boys had already heard about me, and I could tell they were intimidated. I've always been able to spot an intimidated boy—he talks too much, takes cheap shots at my looks, and challenges me right away to see if I'm really as good as they've heard.

What they didn't know was that I had five older brothers. Each of them, in their own way, had prepared me for this moment. They taught me how to be tough, how to throw a punch, how to shoot a basketball, and how to launch a football farther than most boys my age. If I wanted to hang with my brothers and their friends, I had to prove I wasn't soft. You know the saying, *"I can show you better than I can tell you"*? That's exactly what I did. On my first day of flag football, I threw farther, ran faster, and caught better than most of them. Practices and games were filled with the sound of cursing and trash talk—but not one of them ever stepped to me. They knew better. One of my brothers was always nearby, watching.

In middle school, I often found myself asking, "Who am I?" Why was that question so important? Probably because, as the school year unfolded, life came at me fast. I started womanhood, got my first "older" boyfriend, and experienced my first real heartbreak. Looking back, that boy wasn't intelligent—he had one thing on his mind, and it wasn't love. When he realized two things—that I was better than him at sports and that I wasn't giving him what he wanted—he dropped me without hesitation.

These years were also when I discovered something truly special about myself: I had a *musical ear.* I could distinguish between pitches and, as they used to call it back in the day, I could sing *"in the middle."* My music teacher often had me sing off-key in front of the class—not to embarrass me, but to help other students recognize when something was off. Most choirs stick to three-part harmony, but ours sometimes performed in seven: first and second soprano, first and second alto, tenor, baritone, and bass.

My love for music started young—around five or six years old. The church my family attended back then only sang the melody. But I could always hear the harmonies in my head. The challenge? Figuring out how to get them *out*—how to take what I heard inside and translate it into my voice. Funny enough, this ability has passed down to my children. If we hear a song and a harmony comes to us, we *instinctively* sing it. It's second nature to us—but to others, it's probably *incredibly* annoying.

While in middle school, I sang in the school choir, and I'll never forget the first song I learned with harmony—*We Can Work It Out* by The Beatles. As the choir director was teaching the melody to the sopranos, I heard something different in my head—another part, another layer. Without thinking, I started singing it softly under my breath... or so I thought. The director's voice suddenly cut through the room.

"Who is singing that?" she asked.

Caught off guard, I quickly admitted, "It's me. I'm sorry."

But instead of scolding me, she surprised me.

"Sing it again!" she insisted.

I began singing the second line—better known as the alto part—while the sopranos carried the melody. The director paused, clearly intrigued.

"I'm impressed," she said. *"Have you taken lessons?"*

I shook my head. *"No, but I've been singing in the church choir for as long as I can remember."*

That was the moment it clicked—not only did I have an ear for music, but I also had a voice. Growing up, my older siblings and I didn't have a choice when it came to singing in the church choir—we were *voluntold*. But I never protested. I loved music, so I embraced it. I had my first church solo at just five or six years old, but it wasn't until I turned 12 that I truly understood music. Each of these moments shaped me into who I am today. But it took overcoming countless challenges—not just in music, but in life—to truly know and believe that I am exactly who God says I am.

Owning My Judgmental Side

One thing I've learned about myself? I'm judgmental—*on purpose.* How many people can admit that? Sometimes, my judgment comes from a person's appearance. Other times, it's triggered by the way someone exaggerates their achievements. I've never been one to be impressed by money, designer labels, or flashy possessions. Nor am I swayed by people who sound like they learned to talk by flipping through a thesaurus.

I live by a few key principles:

"People use profanity when they can't think of anything intelligent to say."

"I don't use big words unless I know how to use them correctly in a sentence—and actually understand their meaning."

I try to choose my words carefully. I also try not to name-drop. I don't wave my titles or education around for attention. And I certainly don't put a spotlight on my accomplishments unless it's necessary—and even then, I keep it minimal. I firmly believe in the wisdom of *Proverbs 18:16 (NKJV): "A man's gift makes room for him, and brings him before great men."* It may not be the *great men* that others envision, but scripture doesn't specify *who* they will be—only that it *will* happen. I've also found myself being judgmental due to aligning with the wrong people. But that's a conversation for later.

It wasn't until my 40's that I truly began using wisdom and standing up for myself. Before that, I had no problem speaking up for others—if I saw something wrong, I called it out. If I witnessed someone shoplifting, I alerted store personnel. If I found a wallet full of money, I turned it in without hesitation, because I imagined how I would feel if I had lost it. People told me I was foolish for doing the right thing, but to me, integrity always outweighed personal gain.

Speaking up for myself, however, was an entirely different struggle. Whenever I tried, my throat would tighten, my palms would sweat, and anxiety would take over. Confrontation wasn't just about exposing the offender—it meant exposing myself too. And there's a deep, almost paralyzing vulnerability in revealing your pain to others. That fear didn't come from nowhere. It was a seed, likely planted by my mother, who was raised by parents of the Silent Generation. She rarely spoke up, but her actions—or lack thereof—spoke volumes.

Michael Jackson once sang *"Man in the Mirror,"* a song written by Siedah Garrett and Glen Ballard. Its message is powerful—it challenges us to take a hard, honest look at ourselves. Most people glance in the mirror to check their appearance—their outfit, their hair, and their overall look. But how often do we look in the mirror to truly see ourselves? To acknowledge our flaws and ask ourselves how we are contributing to the world—both its rights and its wrongs?

Phil Collins' "*Another Day in Paradise*" speaks volumes about who we are as people. The song tells the story of a woman crying out for help, only to be ignored as a man pretends not to hear her and crosses the street. It makes me reflect on how many times I have done the same—too busy, too distracted, or simply not wanting to be bothered. It wasn't until I imagined myself in their shoes that I realized how easily life can shift. Any of us could be just one prayer away from being in that same situation. My mother never forced us to give to the poor, help an elderly woman across the street, donate to shelters, or to be kind—she simply showed us. Through her actions at work, at church, and in the community, she lived them out daily.

My father was part of what is called the *Greatest Generation*, born two decades before my mother. They weren't the type to talk just for the sake of talking. Their words carried weight and were intentional. They had long, meaningful conversations with each other, but when it came to passing down wisdom to us kids, they kept it short and to the point. Before my father passed, we had a conversation about what to do after he was gone. I asked him, "Daddy, what if I still don't know what to do?" Without hesitation, he responded, "*You'll have to figure it out!*"

Those words still ring in my head almost daily—at work, at church, in my community. It's funny how life throws wisdom back at you when you least expect it. My father wasn't just a man of words; he was a man of action. A U.S. Army veteran, he dedicated his time to serving his community. He quietly gave to causes that mattered—donating to a local nonprofit that promoted equality for African Americans and contributing to cancer research. He didn't talk much about the good he did. He just did it.

I've often been told that I'm someone people can trust with their most sensitive information, and I listen well. I hold their words in confidence. Some call me a "secret keeper." But what most don't realize is that carrying so much knowledge about others and about life can be both a blessing and a burden. It's not as if I dwell on what I've been told or replay it in my mind. Yet, the weight of these unspoken truths is always there, tucked away in a space I never asked to fill.

The responsibility I carry is immense. To betray someone's trust—to share their dreams, fears, health struggles, relationships, or financial hardships—would mean I'm no longer a safe place. And yet, when people realize I know more than a spouse, a best friend, or even a prominent figure, I'm met with criticism, suspicion, and judgment. But if a therapist knows? If a pastor holds the same knowledge? That's acceptable. Is it because I don't have a license? Or is it simply because of who I am? The irony is, if I were to speak, I'd be labeled a gossip or a traitor. But for staying silent, I'm still criticized. Either way, I carry the weight alone.

Earlier this year, I sent an email to a group of people I trusted—both men and women—individuals I knew would be honest with me. I asked them four simple, yet revealing questions:

1. What would you say is my greatest strength?
2. What would you say is one of my biggest weaknesses?
3. If you could hire me for any job, what would it be?
4. What one adjective would you use to describe me?

The reason I asked? Because I often struggle when people say, "Tell me about yourself." It's always been difficult to talk about who I am in a way that feels authentic and complete.

The responses I received were both affirming and eye-opening. Some described me as welcoming, heartwarming, a good listener, and confident. Others noted that, ironically, confidence was also one of my weaknesses—I sometimes fail to see that I'm perfect for a role, even when it's clear to everyone else. Job suggestions ranged from relationship manager to project director.

Other responses pointed to my strong faith in God, my organizational skills, and my ability to communicate effectively. Careers like, Board and Care or Assisted Living were mentioned, and the adjectives used to describe me were nothing short of humbling: dynamic, humble, hardworking, open-minded, optimistic, intelligent, determined, loyal, persistent, remarkable, resilient, reliable, and sincere. Reading these words made me smile. Knowing that people saw me this way was both uplifting and encouraging. But one response hit differently. It was sharp, honest, and, deep down, I knew it was true.

"You are sometimes oblivious to things around you. But that can also be a good thing because it keeps you out of unnecessary mess. The downside? It also causes you to miss things that could prove important." That made me pause. The truth in that last response forced me to reflect on painful moments from my past—moments I once struggled to confront, let alone speak about.

As a child, I was molested by someone my family trusted. I knew what was happening was wrong, but fear kept me silent. I couldn't bring myself to tell an adult. Also, at 16 years old, I found myself in an abusive relationship. Again, I knew it was wrong, but I was too afraid to speak up. Shame played a part—being a victim felt humiliating. But even more than that, I feared no one would believe me. His family was well-known in the community, and I worried that somehow, *I* would be the one blamed.

Looking back, I now understand that my silence wasn't just fear—it was what psychologists and life coaches call a trauma response. I developed a pattern of either saying *too much* about nothing or shutting down completely. Even now, I struggle to voice certain emotions because, deep down, I still battle feelings of being unprotected and unsupported. Many of my most vulnerable moments cost me more than I was ever willing to pay. But healing has changed me. With time and maturity, expressing this side of myself has become easier. It still takes effort, but it no longer feels impossible. I have grown. I have healed.

Unfortunately, witnessing abuse firsthand didn't just affect me emotionally—it also shaped my perceptions of others. It created deep-seated prejudices against people of a certain hue and gender during my early adult years. It took time, reflection, and intentional unlearning to navigate and release those feelings. Now, when a situation triggers memories of the past, the thoughts may surface, but they no longer define me. I acknowledge them, process them, and let them go.

A Moment of Self-EXamination

Through deep self-reflection, I've come to realize that I was then—and I am now—all of those adjectives that were shared with me, and even more. But it has taken years to fully embrace who I am in Christ. I know there is a greater calling on my life, beyond what I am currently doing. I am passionate about my work, yet I often find myself vulnerable to things that seem bigger than me— things that, in reality, are just distractions, the enemy's way of deterring me from my true path.

As I continue to grow, I've had to ask myself some hard questions—ones that challenge me to face my fears, realign my purpose, and seek divine wisdom. Maybe these questions will help you, too:

1. **Who are you—really?**
2. **What or who intimidates you in the spaces you step into?**
3. **What advice would your mother give you?**
4. **What advice would your father give you?**
5. **What would Jesus do?**

The answers may not come easily, but they are worth seeking.

To be honest, my first instinct was to answer question number one with, *"I'm Batman!"*—but that wouldn't be entirely accurate. The truth is, knowing *who you are* is essential—whether you're a person of faith, a member of the military, a community leader, or in any position of influence. Before you can truly help others discover *who they are*, you must first understand yourself.

At your core, you are **mind, will, and emotions.**

Your mind is the thinker—the one that processes, analyzes, and makes sense of the world.

Your will is the decision-maker—the one that chooses the path you take.

Your emotions are the feelers—the ones that respond, react, and connect you to the experiences around you.

Every time you engage with others, there is an exchange—an interaction with your **soul.** Whether it's with your parents, your family, your coworkers, your spouse, or someone you're dating, your soul is always involved. That's why knowing *who you are* isn't just important—it's necessary.

The Cost of Being Judgmental

In my own judgmental ways, I know I've missed out—on meaningful friendships, promising job opportunities, incredible ministry ventures, a good date, and possibly even a great second husband. The truth is, our past shapes how we respond to our future. And while I've healed from many things, one wound remained: trusting people with *me.*

Trust, for me, isn't something I give freely. You might be thinking, *Well, you trust the airplane pilot, the bus driver, the train engineer...* And yes, I do—because I know they aren't personally connected to me. They have no real stake in my life. They're simply doing their jobs. It's business, not personal. But the moment one of them—or anyone else—tries to form a personal relationship with me? My senses go on high alert. And that's when my alter ego, *Elizabeth,* makes her entrance.

Elizabeth and the Art of Flirting

Elizabeth gives me the courage to say things I wouldn't normally say—not anything profane, but definitely bold. Sometimes, she works in my favor. Other times, she gets me into trouble. In my early 20s, I was a *huge* flirt. If I saw a man I found handsome and he wasn't wearing a wedding ring, I was flirting—no hesitation. His race didn't matter. It wasn't about starting anything serious; it was just about seeing what was possible.

One day, I was riding in the passenger seat with one of my sisters when a black Mercedes-Benz with deeply tinted windows pulled up beside us. I could tell the driver was a man, but I couldn't see his face. That didn't stop me. I rolled down my window and, without a second thought, started flirting. The man began rolling his window down in response. Excited, I turned to my sister and said, *"He's interested!"*

And then... *mortification*. It was my *Pastor*. He nodded at me, completely unfazed, and said, *"See you at church."*

I was *done* flirting with strangers. At least for a little while.

Who I Am vs. What I Do

I've often heard the saying, *"Who you are is not what you do."* Your profession—whether an

15

electrician, police officer, firefighter, or city official—is simply a role you fulfill. But *who you truly are* comes from the heart. Scripture reminds us of this truth: *"Out of the abundance of the heart, the mouth speaks."* — Luke 6:45 (KJV). Whatever fills your heart will inevitably spill from your lips. If your heart harbors evil, negativity will flow from your mouth. If your heart is full of kindness, compassion will be your language. While good and evil cannot coexist in the heart, they *can* both be spoken from the same mouth.

For a long time, I've downplayed my gifts—not because I don't recognize them, but because of the attention they bring, both positive and negative. I've played small, even when my gifts were big. But stepping into my *authentic* self means embracing them fully. Financial expert and social media personality *Lynn Richardson*—affectionately known as "Auntie" to many—once said something that stuck with me: *"Don't play small when you have a big gift. Let the light of God shine through you—and give those who can't stand the light a pair of shades."* So, I ask you today—**Who are you?**

Emotional Eating and the Battle Within

When it comes to dealing with anxiety and depression, I turn to food—snacking and overeating have been my go-to coping mechanisms. Chips, ice cream, Mexican food, sandwiches, popcorn, soda—you name it. Mostly salty things. My cravings come in waves, and at this stage in my life, I suspect much of it is hormonal.

If I have to sing a solo—whether in English or Spanish, whether it's a brand-new piece or a song I've sung a hundred times—I get anxious. And when I get anxious, I eat. Ironically, my go-to comfort food is ice cream, the *worst* thing for my throat and vocal cords. It's not fear that drives me to it. I *know* I can sing, and I *know* I can do it well. It's the space *in between*—the waiting, the anticipation—that triggers the behavior. And each time, it plays out the same way. I recognize the trigger *after* I've indulged. That familiar thought creeps in: *"I've done it again."* And with it comes guilt.

The enemy knows our weaknesses better than we do. But acknowledging them is the first step to overcoming them. Engaging in **S.E.X. (Self-EXamination)** means admitting that some battles can't be fought alone. Seeking help—through therapy, group discussions, prayer, and healthier coping strategies—starts the healing process in the right direction. Healing doesn't begin when we're perfect—it begins when we're honest.

The Battle with Imposter Syndrome

I've wrestled with **Imposter Syndrome** for as long as I can remember. It sneaks into multiple areas of my life—especially my singing. But it doesn't stop there. It affects my willingness to be active, to take on physical challenges like running another marathon. I *know* I can do it, yet I downplay my abilities as if I can't. It seeps into my work, my writing, and nearly everything I know I do exceptionally well.

According to *Management30.com*, there are **five types of Imposter Syndrome**:

1. **The Perfectionist** – Expects everything to go flawlessly. Even a small mistake feels like complete failure.
2. **The Superhero** – Measures success by juggling multiple roles. Falling short in any of them feels like failure.
3. **The Expert** – Feels the need to *know everything*. Any gap in knowledge equates to incompetence.
4. **The Natural Genius** – Expects to achieve high goals effortlessly. Struggles feel like a personal shortcoming.
5. **The Soloist** – Prefers to do everything alone. Asking for help feels like weakness.

The common thread? **Failure.** Or at least the *perception* of failure. I relate to three of these. But my hesitation in admitting them comes from a deep fear—what if someone uses this against me? What if they take my vulnerability as an opportunity to judge me?

Questions to Consider:

1. Do you struggle with **Imposter Syndrome**?
2. Which type(s) do you identify with?

3. Now that you know, what are you going to do about it?
4. Do you believe in therapy? Why or why not?
5. What are your triggers?

One of our former church leaders—someone I considered a father figure—passed away in 2023. He and I had countless conversations about life, and one thing he often called me was a **perfectionist**. Each time he said that to me, I gave him the *side-eye* because I knew he was right. At first, I took it as an insult. But as I learned more about the term, I realized not only was he spot-on—he recognized himself in me. *Game recognizes game.*

Chapter Two

S.E.X. Patron – What Am I Contributing To?

How Am I Contributing?

There are worse things in life than being diagnosed with breast cancer—*twice.* One of them is never embracing who you truly are. Another? Squandering opportunities, resources, and blessings—like spending **$26.2 million** in lottery winnings on luxury cars you'll never drive, houses you'll never live in, and clothes you'll never wear, all while refusing to give back, invest wisely, or make a meaningful impact.

Take tithing, for example. Some winners cringe at the idea of giving *10%* of their earnings to a church, believing it's too much. But let's do the math—10% of **$26.2 million** is **$2.620,000 Million**. That still leaves **$24 million** in their pockets. And yet, some would rather keep it all, never considering the blessings that come with generosity.

Then there's the irresponsibility of ignoring past debts. Imagine having the money to pay off every bill you once struggled with—but instead, you let them pile up as if your financial burdens magically disappeared with a lottery win. Or worse—the ones who always make sure *they* are dressed to impress, looking like they just stepped out of a designer showroom, while their children look neglected, as if they belong in a telethon commercial for the unhoused. We all contribute to something—whether good or bad, purposeful or wasteful. The question is: **What are you contributing to? And how?** Not just financially, but in every aspect of life.

It wasn't until **1994** that I began tithing regularly to my church. At first, I tithed off my *net* income—let's be honest, because it meant giving a smaller amount. But after feeling convicted and realizing that God *could* have asked for **20%**, I made a commitment to tithe off my *gross* income, no matter what that meant.

If I received birthday money, I tithed.
If I won a contest, I tithed.
If I was on welfare or receiving unemployment benefits, I tithed.

This isn't a chapter about tithing—it's about self-reflection. It's about asking ourselves: **What am I contributing to? And how?** I once heard a preacher say, *"If you want to know what you truly* *value, check your bank statement."* That may not be 100% accurate for everyone, but it *should* make you think.

There is a powerful story in the Bible, **John 9:1-11** talks about a man who was born blind. The disciples, seeing his condition, asked Jesus whether his blindness was the result of his own sin or the sins of his parents. But Jesus answered, *"Neither this man nor his parents sinned, but that the works of God should be revealed in him."* It was believed that if he could make it into the **Pool of Siloam**, he would be healed. Every day, people rushed to the pool and were miraculously restored from various infirmities. Yet, this man **sat by the pool for 38 years** and never got in.

This made me wonder: *"Did he truly want to change his situation? Did he really want to be healed?"* I imagine he did, yet Scripture never mentions him making an effort to reach the water. Instead, he states that no one was willing to help him get there.

Jesus didn't just tell him to get up and go—He **took action**. He spat on the ground, mixed His saliva with the dirt, and made clay. Then, He anointed the blind man's eyes with it and told him, *"Go, wash in the Pool of Siloam."* The man obeyed—and his sight was restored. This story serves as a reminder: Sometimes, healing doesn't come the way we expect. It requires faith, obedience, and a willingness to move when Jesus says, *"Go."*

Do You Really Want to Be Healed?

Thirty-eight years is a long time to wait for something without making the effort to reach for it. I don't have more details about this man's story, but it makes me wonder. As a two-time cancer survivor, if I knew my healing was in that pool, I would do whatever it took to get there—no excuses. So why didn't he? Maybe he *didn't* truly want to be healed. Some people don't want change because staying a victim feels easier. Others want change but don't know *how* to make it happen. Then, there are those who *do* know what to do but refuse to act. Some crave attention. Some prefer to be a distraction rather than take responsibility for their own healing. When it comes to healing, sometimes *all we need to do is ask.*

It makes me wonder—did Jesus want the man to say, *"I want to be healed"*? Some might argue, *"Well, if He's Jesus, He already knew that."* And they'd be right. But **asking** is an act of participation. It's a demonstration of faith, not just passive waiting. Before Jesus showed up, this man had spent years contributing to his own stagnation instead of his restoration. The truth is, each of us has something that needs healing. But healing requires action. It requires us to ask for help—and to take part in the process. There were times when I wanted to take credit for my own healing instead of giving the glory to Jesus. I made it about *me* instead of *Him*. And in doing so, I believe I offended the Healer.

The Power of Self-EXamination

I firmly believe that people learn best when they seek help for themselves. Growth, healing, and transformation require active participation. Whether you believe it or not, there are people who would rather see you remain stuck—sick, broken, and unproductive. Some thrive on keeping others down because it makes them feel superior. That's why **Self-EXamination** is so important. Take a moment and ask yourself these questions:

- **Do you identify with the man at the pool?** Are you waiting for something to happen instead of making an effort to change?
- **Are you actively contributing to your healing, or are you standing in your own way?**
- **Are you surrounding yourself with the wrong people, entertaining negative thoughts, or walking in the wrong purpose?**
- **Do you have a "my way or no way" mentality?** Are you the type to say, *"If it's not done my way, then it can't be done"?* If so, reconsider your approach. Better yet, ask someone you trust to give you honest feedback—like I did—and listen to what they say.
- **Do you believe you don't need Self-EXamination to improve?** Whether the feedback you receive is good, bad, or

indifferent, accept it with humility. Take what you need to grow, and leave the rest for God to sort out. When we give credit to the *wrong* source, we dishonor the *Ultimate* source—God.

- **What do you really want Jesus to do for you?** Have you even asked?
- **Are you truly willing to do what it takes to receive your healing?**
- **How will you take part in your own healing? Where will you start?**
- **Are you unknowingly contributing to dysfunction?** Are you controlling? Do you only want people around when they serve *your* needs? Are you self-centered or emotionally draining?

The first step to healing is recognizing where you stand. The next step? **Doing something about it.**

An Honest Apology and a Truthful Confession

Let me take a moment to apologize to any woman I've crossed paths with who may have felt I was flirting with her man. That was never my intention. You see, I *thrive* on intellectual stimulation from the opposite sex. I naturally gravitate toward men who make me *think*, who challenge my mind, who spark curiosity and exploration—not *of them*, but of ideas, knowledge, and perspectives.

For me, it's not about attraction, it's about *engagement.* I also crave intellectual depth, not romantic pursuit. Sometimes, books, movies, music, and even numbers can satisfy that need. But nothing—and I mean *nothing*—fires up my brain like deep, thought-provoking conversations with a man who has something meaningful to say. If our conversation is limited to **bills, problems, your kids, my kids, financial struggles, or gaming**, I'll be checked out before we even get past the first topic. You'll be left with a hollow version of me, silently regretting that I didn't take a different path in that moment. And let's be real—it is a *fact* that we **need** men. Yes, I said it! But let me also be clear: *not everything that glitters is gold.*

Let's Talk About Invisible Lint

Ladies, let's be real for a second. You know what I'm talking about—**invisible lint.** That *convenient excuse* to touch a man's coat, his collar, his arm… all while pretending it's completely innocent.

"Oh, let me get that off you." Except there's nothing there.

I can already hear y'all reacting. Don't come for me—I used to do it too. But let's bring it back to the **real** question of this chapter: **What are you contributing to? And how are you contributing?** If I haven't made it clear already, I've only been walking in wisdom for the last **10 to 12 years.** Before that? Let's just say I was *learning*—and I'm tryin' to help somebody now! Now, let me switch gears for a moment. I have a question: **Does God say, "Amen"?**

Think about it. Does He really? My father used to say, *"And so it is."* But that wasn't necessarily a *yes*—it was more like, *"That's the way it is."* But is it really? Is it really what *it* is? Or is it what *you* want it to be because you don't want to admit what it actually *is*? This phrase—*"It is what it is"*—gets abused. People use it to avoid responsibility, to pass the buck, to run from the truth. But if you take a moment to really examine *what "it" is,* you might realize... *it's exactly what you made it.*

Lessons from Dating a Smoker & Childhood News Sources

When I was in my 20s, I dated a man who was a smoker. I *really* liked him, so I convinced myself that I could eventually get him to quit. Spoiler alert: It didn't work. When I write out my list of qualities I want in a future husband, *non-smoker* is non-negotiable. **Here's why:**

1. **I'm a two-time cancer survivor.** Smoke and I don't mix—I have allergies, and I refuse to put my health at risk.
2. **Kissing a smoker feels like kissing a cigarette.** The taste, the smell—it's just *not* for me.
3. **Smoking isn't healthy.** If you're a smoker, it means you're making a conscious choice not to take care of your body.

I understand that people smoke for different reasons—stress, anxiety, depression, weight loss, or just as a coping mechanism. I'm not judging; I'm just sharing my personal preferences.

How We Got Our News as Kids

Back in the day, my version of *"morning news"* came from the back of a cereal box at breakfast. Family meetings? We didn't have those. We didn't sit around discussing current events, war, racism, or slavery—unless our parents chose to bring it up. We learned by *listening* rather than *asking.* Occasionally, we'd get a chance to read the newspaper, but let's be honest—we weren't flipping through looking for world news. We were there for one thing: The comics. Or as we used to call them, *"the funny papers."*

A Hard Truth About Helping Others

I once met a woman—a single mother with three children, all under the age of ten. She desperately needed a place to stay, and I was able to help her secure an emergency housing voucher. She refused it because she didn't like the neighborhood it was in. That moment taught me a hard lesson. There was a time when I would go out of my way to **convince, encourage, or even push** people like her to accept help—to take shelter rather than sleep in a car or a crowded shelter. But I don't do that anymore. Why? Because it doesn't make sense to argue with someone who is broke or homeless—yet refuses help because it doesn't meet their personal preferences.

It also baffles me when someone is offered money or a safe place to stay, but they turn it down because of **pride, fear, or unrealistic expectations.** And yet, I've come to realize that **part of the blame falls on me, too.** It's my fault because I'm part of a society that has let people down before. To that woman, I probably represented **someone or something that reminded her of past disappointments**—a time when she was hurt, manipulated, or tricked into trusting the wrong person, only for it to backfire. At the same time, **it was also her fault.** At some point, **we all have to take responsibility for our own healing and growth.** She had a chance to change her circumstances. Someone she claimed to trust presented her with a solution, and she **chose** not to take it. Healing, progress, and transformation **require action.** No one else can do that part for us.

Chapter Three

The S.E.X. Talk

It Is My Fault & It Is Their Fault

Speaking uncomfortable truths is never easy, but it's necessary. Even if the only one you can confide in is God—have the conversation.

Growing up, my siblings and I often walked home from school. Along the way, there was a stretch we called **"the woods."** It wasn't a forest, but it might as well have been. Towering trees loomed over the path, their thick trunks and dense branches stretching toward the sky, blocked out the sunlight. Though the walk through the woods wasn't long, it always felt **endless** when I was alone.

To distract myself from being afraid, I would sing. The sound of my own voice was comforting, a way to fill the silence. As I walked, I would tilt my head back, searching for a glimpse of blue sky through the treetops. If I could see even the smallest patch of blue, it made me feel less alone. Walking through the woods was unsettling enough on a bright, sunny day—so you can imagine how terrifying it was when the sky was overcast or when I found myself there just before sundown. Those solitary walks became something more than just a fearful journey home. They became moments of prayer, reflection, and conversation with God.

One day, as I walked through the woods, I realized something—I was alone **because of my own choices.** I had lingered at school too long, and now I was paying the price for it. My mother **worried about us** when my sister and I had to walk home alone. It was during a time when child abductions were on the rise, and she lived in constant fear that something awful would happen to us. Leaving school late meant getting home late. And getting home late meant one thing— **Momma was not happy.**

As punishment, I wasn't allowed to go to my friend's house to hang out. For some, that might not sound like a real consequence, but for a **social butterfly** like me, it was *torture.* Even if I had a legitimate reason to shift the blame onto someone else, it didn't matter. I wasn't allowed to. My mother made sure I owned my part in it even if, in some twisted way, that simply meant accepting the fact that I existed.

Owning My Choices—Even the Immature Ones

You might think the first story was **immature**, and you'd be right. But I was *immature* when I made that decision. The truth is, even now—older and (supposedly) wiser—I still make **immature** choices. The difference? **I own up to them.**

I've been blessed to have *seasoned* men and women pour wisdom into my life for as long as I can remember. Many of them gave me solid, practical advice—simple guidance that, had I followed, would have saved me from unnecessary pain. But sometimes, learning the hard way is the only way.

The Magnet Incident

As a child, I had a bad habit of putting strange things in my mouth and chewing on them. My mother constantly warned me not to—worried I'd choke. When I was about six years old, I was getting out of the bathtub with a small **magnet** in my mouth. It was shaped like a cylinder and about a half inch long. I was swishing it around like candy. I ran and jumped into a fresh, warm pile of laundry on the couch—right out of the dryer. In that moment, I accidentally swallowed the magnet. Panic set in immediately. I jumped up and ran to my mother who was in the kitchen frying chicken. I was pointing frantically at my throat to let her know I was choking.

Back then, we didn't know anything about the Heimlich Maneuver. My mother did the only thing she could think of—she repeatedly patted my back, hoping to dislodge it. But the magnet wouldn't budge. Instead, I felt it moving *slowly* down my throat, causing pain and discomfort. She rushed me to the Emergency Room where they took X-rays. The images showed that the magnet had traveled further—it was now stuck in my chest. The doctors were concerned, but they told us the same thing over and over: *"It should pass on its own."* They sent me home with **pain medication** and told us to *wait*. That was it. Just *wait*.

For days, I experienced sharp discomfort and found myself spitting constantly. The doctors later explained that the metal in my body was likely causing the excessive saliva production. To this day, I have no idea when or if that magnet ever passed. But what I do know? My **disobedience** caused me unnecessary pain. And worse? **It caused my mother fear. Yes, it was my fault.**

Taylor Swift Was Right—"I'm the Problem, It's Me"

Taylor Swift said it best in her song *Anti-Hero*: **"I'm the problem, it's me."** Looking back at the last ten jobs I've had, there's been a pattern—**opposition from day one.** Every time I started a new position, I was met with challenges, resistance, and, at times, outright war. And more often than not, the conflict came from **women— primarily women of the same race.** Some of them were corporate leaders, the very people who hired me. Others were employees I was responsible for supervising.

At one job, I was **fired** simply for attempting to hold someone accountable. I wanted to write up a staff member for repeated **insubordination**, but I was warned that doing so could cause *"irreversible damage"* and create a bigger issue. That moment forced me to question my own role: *How can I be hired for a position where I have power—but no authority?* It was frustrating, disheartening, and humbling. Before I lost that job, I had already prayed. I asked God to show me what to do next—to prepare me for my next *assignment.* And as always, He answered.

Strange Harmonies in the Workplace

Many of the staff members in that former job displayed **narcissistic** and **passive-aggressive** behaviors—two traits I've learned *never* to trust. Beyond that, the workplace itself had an unsettling **cult-like** environment. Everyone seemed to be fighting for "Daddy's" attention. Meetings often turned into a competition, with employees one-upping each other: *"Well, I did this last week..." "I finished this ahead of schedule..." "Look at everything I accomplished..."* It was a constant performance, a desperate attempt to outshine the next person—a pattern I like to call **"Strange Harmonies."**

As a singer, I know that **dissonance**—clashing or unresolved notes—can be intentional in music.

When used correctly, it adds depth to a song. But when a **wrong** note is randomly thrown into a perfectly structured chord, it creates *chaos* instead of harmony. And that's exactly what this environment felt like—a constant, jarring clash in the middle of something that should have made sense.

Recognizing the Real Problem

Not too long ago, I had the opportunity to see a former boss—the one who made my time under her difficult. But God shielded me. At one point, our eyes locked, but she didn't recognize me. I, however, knew exactly who she was. God is funny like that. Sometimes, He allows you to see your **enemies**—not just for the sake of seeing them, but to reveal the **consequences of their own actions.** That woman looked older than her years—fragile, worn down. The same person who once stood in authority over me now looked as though life had humbled her. I always knew that gender and race played a role in the way certain people treated me. But that was their issue, not mine.

These power struggles and petty competitions usually began within the first week of meeting them. So, I often found myself asking God: *"Why am I here?"*

"What is wrong with them?" *"What is wrong with me?"* Seeking wisdom, I turned to a trusted friend for advice. His response shook me:

"You're the problem." I was dumbfounded.

"Excuse me?" I asked.

He explained, *"You're the problem because when you walk into a room, you bring Christ with you. People see there's something different about you— something they can't quite place. And often, it's something they don't like. They can already tell— you ain't the one."* That made me pause.

More than once, people have asked if I served in the military. Maybe it's the way I walk—upright, confident. Maybe it's the way I dress—always in **business attire** at work. Maybe it's because I try to run a **tight ship.** *Too* tight for some, I suppose. My response was always the same: *"No, I didn't serve in the military, but I wanted to. I dress for the job I want, not the job I have. And more than anything, I carry the discipline my mother and grandmother instilled in me."* Those conversations made me question myself. *Was I expecting too much? Was my level of discipline unrealistic?* A man who was like a father figure to me used to say, "You'd better get it right, or you'll hear from Ms. Laura." At first, I laughed whenever he said it. But after some reflection, I realized the truth behind his words—I was asking a lot of people who didn't have a lot to give. One of my mentors often said, "People don't know what they don't know." And that's the reality. You can't expect people to rise to a standard they've never been taught.

Sound It Out—The Power of Phonics and Persistence

As a kid, we were taught to read using by using phonics. Any time I struggled with a word, my teachers and my mother would say, *"Sound it out!"* Once I mastered that skill, there wasn't a word I couldn't pronounce or read. Okay, nerd alert...With my newfound confidence, I proudly became the first among my siblings to learn how to spell a big word—*antidisestablish-mentarianism.* And I was only nine years old.

If you break it down, the word itself contains at least five smaller words—probably more. But phonics made it possible to tackle even the most intimidating words, and I still use that strategy today. Here's the real kicker—I didn't just learn to read early, I learned to read fluently by the age of four. My mother took full advantage of this. She would have me read everything—labels on boxes, cans, magazines, and of course, the Bible. She loved hearing me read, and looking back, it was her way of sharpening my diction and articulation.

I read cereal boxes, street signs, license plates—anything with words. Whether at home, watching television, or riding in the backseat of the car, I was constantly sounding out words, both in my head and out loud. I never realized my mother was paying such close attention until one day, I hit a roadblock. We came across a street sign that stumped me—*Francisquito*. With full confidence, I pronounced it *"Squiddo."*

My mother quickly corrected me: *"The 'Qu' is pronounced like a 'K' sound."*

In my head, I was *annoyed. "Well, why didn't they just spell it with 'Sk' so people like me—who love reading—wouldn't get stumped?"* But that moment taught me something valuable: "Practice makes better—not perfect." Because when we keep trying, when we apply effort with intention, we will always improve.

Tradition, Growth, and the Waves We Make

I come from a traditional family—one rooted in traditional values, church rules, and God-honoring behaviors. And while I'm not saying those things aren't important, I *am* saying they shouldn't hold you back from progressing.

I once heard a man say, *"If we continue to do things the way we've always done them, they will die."* And he was right. Evolution requires movement. It means stepping forward, embracing the new, and slowly shedding the old mindsets that keep us stagnant. **Hebrews 11** speaks to this—faith is about moving forward, *even when you don't see the whole picture.* Refusing to evolve is like telling God, *"I'm good just the way I am"* *when you aren't.*

Am I Approachable?

I prided myself on being easy to talk to—someone you can have a real conversation with. But I've realized some people don't know the difference between being approachable and being available. Maybe they hesitate because they're unsure of how to approach me. Maybe they've already made up their minds about who I am. Maybe...they're just afraid. Let me be clear—I've *always* been approachable. That hasn't changed. What *has* changed? I'm just more private now. There's a difference.

Making Bigger Waves

The impact of my parents and grandparents still ripples through my life today. The waves *they* made are still moving us. So, ask yourself this:

Are you being tossed around, waiting for the storm to pass? Or are you stepping up to make bigger waves—pushing forward, refusing to stay where you are, even when it's uncomfortable? Holding on just to survive is one thing. Making waves that create change? That's another.

Lessons in Leadership: Educate, Delegate, Motivate, Terminate

I've been fortunate to have rare conversations with men and women who hold far more wisdom and experience than I do. One such conversation stood out—an encounter with a stranger where I shared my struggles. I told him how, time and time again, I faced challenges when stepping into new jobs, ministries, or community roles. His response was simple yet profound: *"You have to categorize people and leadership techniques.*

The categories are:

1. **Educate** – If they don't know, **teach** them. Give them the knowledge they need to succeed.
2. **Delegate** – Once they've learned, **give them something to do**. Let them take responsibility.
3. **Motivate** – If they start to struggle, **encourage them**. Remind them, *"You can do this."*
4. **Terminate** – If you've **educated, delegated, and motivated**—yet they still refuse to improve or put in the effort—**let them go.** Terminate the job, the relationship, or the leadership role.

That advice changed my perspective. Since hearing it, I've made it a guiding principle in how I interact with all people. I've chosen not to hesitate, not to agitate, but to rehabilitate.

A Moment of Vulnerability: The Night God Met Me in My Darkness

I remember one of the darkest nights of my life. It was after work in **2018**, and I was completely overwhelmed. I felt like I had been fighting for so long, only to keep losing. I didn't want to keep going. I didn't want to feel anymore. I didn't want to die by my own hands—I just wanted God to take me in my sleep. Everything was my fault—or so I had been told. And worse? I believed it. I felt like I had no support. I felt like God didn't care. *Or so I thought.* But **God.**

Through my tears, I cried out to Him, broken and exhausted—asking *why* over and over again. My face was soaked, my shirt drenched from the flood of tears and emotions I could no longer hold back. I laid down, waiting. Waiting to fall asleep, waiting to slip away. And then, something happened.

A bright light appeared in my room—so bright, it was almost blinding. I wiped my face and just stared at the light. I knew, without a doubt, **God had come to see about me.** In that moment, He gave me a **vision.** I jumped up, ran to my computer, and started typing. I typed everything He showed me, every detail He placed on my heart. By the time I was done, I had eight pages of revelation. Eight pages of purpose. Eight pages of reasons to keep going. The Holy Spirit became my covering—my *top sheet*—shielding me from the enemy's prickly blanket of doubt, fear, and sorrow. I praised God for the blessing of **life** and the vision that saved me. But I also had to face a hard truth. It was their fault—for allowing themselves to be used by the enemy to speak negativity over me.

But it was also my fault.

- My fault for believing the enemy's lies.
- My fault for removing my *top sheet*—for allowing myself to be exposed to pain and deception.
- My fault for letting others dictate my happiness instead of trusting the One who gave it to me in the first place.

But that night changed everything because when I was at my lowest, God reminded me who I was. And that was enough for me to keep going.

Conditional Apologies, Conversational Narcissism & Knowing When to Walk Away

There was a time when some of the very people who offended me came back to apologize. Or at least, that's what they *thought* they were doing. Instead of leading with **"I apologize"** or **"I messed up"**, they started with **"If."**

"If I hurt you... If I offended you... If I did something wrong..." That's not an apology. That's a conditional statement. A real apology doesn't require you to validate their wrongs before they take accountability. It doesn't require you to explain why you were hurt just so they can decide if they *actually* did something wrong. The only time **"if"** holds power is when Jesus used it in scripture:

"If I be lifted up..."

"If my people who are called by my name..."

"If thou let this cup pass from me…"

Any other "if" is not official.

Conversational Narcissism: The Art of Making Everything About You

Another way people become the problem is by hijacking someone's moment and turning it into their own.

It's called **conversational narcissism. Here is an example:**
"Girl, I'm really going through it right now. I need prayer."

Their response? *"Girl, me too. Last week I was checking my bank account and I'm broke. I might lose my job, my house, and I don't know what I'm gonna do. My mother is this. My father is that. My neighbor did this. And so on, and so on…"* And suddenly, the conversation never returns to the *original person* who asked for support. Then, at the very end, they throw in the classic line: **"Well, I'll keep you in my prayers."** *Pray for what, exactly?* You weren't even **listening** in the first place!

Defending Yourself Against Insecurities That Aren't Yours

I get tired of defending myself in spaces where my loyalty, friendship, dedication, and character have been proven for decades. What usually happens? Someone else's **insecurities** take hold, and instead of dealing with them, they **project them onto me.** Suddenly, I'm being blamed for things I had **nothing to do with.** And before I know it, I'm spending **way too much time** trying to convince people of a truth they *should* already know.

And because their voice carries weight, I become the victim of a character assassination. The wildest part? It's not just an *attempt* at assassination. It's **a full-blown execution.** Relationships I once thought were strong and solid start to crumble. People I believed in start distancing themselves—not because of what I did, but because of what *they heard.* And that leaves me wondering: Were those relationships ever truly strong and loyal in the first place?

If they were, why were they so easily convinced to turn their backs on me?

Knowing When to Cut People Off

I was listening to a podcast where a female speaker talked about cutting certain people out of her life because they weren't contributing to her growth or aligning with what God had for her. Her best friend responded:

"My cut-off game is back. It was worse back then than it is now." That made me reflect—I'm the opposite. As a kid, my *cut-off game* was horrible because I wanted to be friends with everybody. I was playful, social, and got along with just about anyone I met. It wasn't until I got my first job that my mother told me something that changed my perspective: **"Everybody who smiles in your face is not your friend."** Now *that* was a word.

The older I get, the more I value my solitude. But that solitude comes with mixed emotions. Part of me doesn't like going places alone—I'm a people-oriented person. The other part? I don't have anyone to go with me. And then there's the reality of the world we live in. Sometimes, I don't want to be outside because there's *too much going on*—too much danger, too much negativity. And to be honest? I don't want to get kidnapped, jumped, beaten, or robbed. I also have trust issues. Psychologists call it a **"trauma response."** And while I know this isn't the best way to live, this is where I am right now. It's my hope that I can become more extroverted again—that I can step outside of these walls more freely. But I also know... it's going to take a push.

A Lesson in Workplace Politics & Professional Betrayal

I once had an African American female supervisor whom I deeply admired. She had climbed the ranks quickly and was well-respected in her field. I was impressed by her success and inspired by her story, wanting to follow in her footsteps.

When she hired me, she told me, "This is your ship. Run it as you see fit."

But what she really meant was, the ship was hers—mine was just the little tugboat being pulled along behind it.

False Promises & Workplace Reality

During my interview conversations, I expressed interest in reaching the 'C-Suite' someday. My supervisor confidently said, "I can help you with that." We seemed to have made a connection—as *Sistahs* and colleagues. But as time went on, I would come to learn that our "connection" was just an illusion.

A Rough Start

When I arrived at my new office, I was greeted by my Assistant. She, too, was an African American female. I spoke first, "Hi. I'm Laura." She seemed a little bothered by me. Her response to my introduction was, "There's the office" pointing to the right, and she handed me my set of keys. The office was in complete disarray—dusty, stale-smelling, and clearly neglected since the COVID-19 shutdown. As my week moved on, I realized that the Assistant I inherited was lazy, unprofessional, and very disrespectful. Still, I was determined to make it work.

We wore masks and barely interacted unless it was absolutely necessary. Our job descriptions were clear, but every time I asked for help while adjusting to the company's processes, my assistant would respond with:

- *"Are your hands broken?"*
- *"Can't you get it yourself?"*

I quickly realized that this wasn't going to be easy.

Thrown Into the Deep End

Navigating two new software programs was challenging, and I repeatedly sought guidance from my supervisor and coworkers. But the support I received was minimal at best. Most responses boiled down to:

"Figure it out."

The phrase hit me hard—reminding me of a conversation I had with my father as a child when I asked, *"What if I don't know what to do?"* and he simply replied, *"Figure it out."*

Desperate for help, I reached out to colleagues who initially offered assistance—but when the time came, their help was half-hearted at best.

After a few months, I began to see the company's true culture.

The "Cult-Like" Corporate Culture

This was a small but wealthy company—they owned multiple buildings, had a tight-knit leadership team, and only about 75 employees.

They paid well, primarily because they owned what they managed, allowing them to keep the money in-house. But Monday meetings revealed an odd power dynamic—staff members constantly competed for "Daddy's" attention.

- If one person accomplished something, another would immediately try to one-up them.
- It wasn't about teamwork—it was about winning favor with the higher-ups.

It was bizarre, but I wasn't about to quit just because of some opposition.

Going the Extra Mile—Only to Be Undermined

I pushed myself to go above and beyond.

✓ My commute was **30 miles each way**.

✓ My shift was **8 AM to 5 PM**, yet I would arrive **by 7:15 AM** and stay until **6 PM**.

✓ As a junior supervisor, I was on salary, meaning no overtime—yet I worked extra hours anyway because there was so much to do.

At one point, my supervisor asked me for ideas to strengthen staff connections. I eagerly provided engaging team-building activities, including:

✓ **Partner-based games to encourage collaboration**

✓ **A White Elephant gift exchange**

✓ **A "Who Am I?" game using baby pictures and childhood summaries**

She loved the ideas—but when we met with corporate leadership, she did a complete 180.

She publicly called me out, saying: *"If it's not Laura's way, it's the highway."* Not only was this completely false, but it was humiliating. She also blamed me for the lack of cohesiveness within my team—despite the fact that I was still new to the company and adjusting.

A Shift in the Air

I had unknowingly made a mistake that sealed my fate. During a corporate conference, we were discussing future aspirations. My supervisor mentioned her dream of writing a memoir. In an innocent effort to connect, I casually shared: *"I've written a few books—they're available on Amazon."* Big mistake. I didn't realize it at the time, but after that day, her attitude toward me changed.

The Silent Plot to Push Me Out

Over the next few months, I faced mounting opposition from both my supervisor and my assistant. An awkward tension settled between us, but I didn't fully grasp what was happening behind the scenes. My supervisor was strategically trying to get rid of me—but doing so in a way that seemed *"respectable."*

The Betrayal

One of my other staff members was repeatedly insubordinate—both privately and publicly. Following company policy, **I reported the issue** to my supervisor, and she instructed me to *"Write her up."* So I did.

✓ I carefully **documented a timeline** of every incident.

✓ Before issuing the write-up, I **emailed it to my supervisor** for review.

✓ I followed up with a **phone call**, seeking **guidance on presenting it.**

After reading it, my supervisor told me to hold off until she could discuss it with her higher-ups. I waited. Two days later, when I finally got in touch with her again—I was the one getting written up.

A Blindsiding Write-Up

There was no warning. No indication that I had done anything wrong. Yet here I was, receiving a four-page-long disciplinary write-up.

✓ It listed bullet points from A to W—a laundry list of fabricated issues and exaggerated concerns.
✓ It was clear—she had been building a case against me all along.

At that moment, I realized the entire system was rigged. My supervisor had never intended to mentor me or help me climb the ranks. Instead, she was protecting her own position—and I had unknowingly become a threat. I also discovered that the reason my Assistant was disrespectful towards me is because she wanted the promotion prior to me being hired. Unfortunately, before I was let go, she was fired for falsifying records.

Final Thoughts

Looking back, this experience taught me a hard but valuable lesson:

✓ Not everyone who looks like you will look out for you.

✓ Some people fear your success more than they support your growth.

✓ Being competent, confident, and driven makes you a target in certain environments.

✓ Toxic workplaces disguise themselves as opportunity-rich spaces—until you realize they're designed to keep you in your place.

I walked away wiser, stronger, and with a renewed understanding of how workplace politics truly operate. I may have lost the job, but I gained clarity—and *that* is priceless.

The End of a Marriage & The Beginning of Clarity

I was legally married for 16 years and 9 months. But in reality, my marriage ended at 15 years and 3 months—when we separated. I vividly remember the conversation about taking time apart—not as an ending, but as a way to heal individually and then come back together for counseling. The goal was to fix what was broken, rebuild, and move forward stronger. My spouse acknowledged that our marriage had major issues, but he refused to agree to a separation. I knew we needed space—a chance to breathe, reflect, and reset. But in the end, I was the only one who took that opportunity. For over seven years, we cycled through seven different pastors and counselors, including our own, with no success. We were stuck in an endless loop.

"God Hates Divorce" – A Verse Misunderstood

When I suggested a separation, my spouse's response was **instant and forceful**:

"God hates divorce!" He was quoting **Malachi 2:16**, which says: *"For the Lord, the God of Israel, says that He hates divorce."* I had heard that verse countless times, and for years, I feared it. I didn't want to disobey God. I didn't want to break His heart. And, above all, I didn't want our five children to suffer because of my decision. But after I separated, I **sought Christian counseling from an unbiased pastor**—someone outside of my church who could **speak to my situation objectively**. This pastor **reframed the verse for me** in a way I had never heard before:

"God hates divorce the same way He would hate seeing someone's head being decapitated." "Not only is it painful for the person involved, but it also creates a mess for everyone around them." God doesn't want His children to suffer—not in broken marriages, and not in bitter divorces. Once I had that visual, I finally understood.

The Moment I Knew It Was Over

In the first month of separation, I still believed we could fix our marriage. By the morning of my birthday, just six weeks later, I knew the truth: We weren't getting back together. Accepting that reality was hard—not just because of the life I had known, but because of the weight of perception. We were both leaders in our church, and I dreaded the thought of the congregation knowing we were separated. I asked my spouse if we could "keep up the act" until he felt comfortable enough to sit somewhere else in the sanctuary. He agreed.

The Final Confirmation

Our pastor agreed to counsel us separately for six months. At the end of that time, we would come back together to reevaluate and decide whether to continue the marriage. We both agreed to the process. But by the time those six months had passed, I had made up my mind.

✓ I had done the work.

✓ He had not.

✓ I was done.

Sitting in our pastor's office, I had a moment of clarity—I had been hoping for change, but nothing had changed. Shortly after, my spouse chose a new seat in the sanctuary. And just like that, the performance was over. I was no longer embarrassed. I was no longer worried about appearances. I had made my decision—and I was at peace with it. I had made my bed—and I was prepared to lie in it.

Questions to Ponder

1. **Who you are in agreement with is a reflection of where you are headed.**
2. **Cliques and Clowns. Gossip and Slander.** Maybe you should reevaluate *why* you're in certain relationships.
3. **Was the foundation of that relationship shaky or strong?**
4. **Should you sever old ties to establish new, healthier connections?**
5. **When you're hurting, tired, or in trouble—what do you turn to?**
6. **Are you holding on to a relationship that should have ended?**
7. **Have you had the same challenge with a colleague that had the same results?**

The answers to these questions will tell you more than you know.

Chapter Four

S.E.X. Acts

What Are You Gonna Do About It?

I was watching an episode of *Sweet Magnolias* on Netflix when a character said, *"Pain inspires a lot of unhealthy decisions."* That statement resonated deeply.

Our relationship with Jesus Christ is not an *à la carte* option—something we pick and choose based on convenience. Yet, within the Black community, we often find ourselves wrestling with topics that are deemed off-limits or whispered about in secret. Conversations about plastic surgery, hair coloring, diet choices—fried foods versus veganism—are minor compared to the weightier struggles: divorce and singleness, domestic violence, sexual assault, molestation, addiction, mental health, and the stigma that silences us. We whisper our diagnoses as if speaking to them aloud gives them power. Sometimes, not even our hairdresser knows what we're battling. But the question remains—what are we going to do about it?

I was five years old when I witnessed my first act of violence. My mother was chasing my brother through the backyard with a belt. She was nearly as fast as he was. Though he outran her, she outsmarted him—pausing just long enough to change direction, circling around the tree in the yard, and cutting him off. In the end, he got his butt whooped anyway.

The second act of violence I witnessed was when I was nine, living in Los Angeles, CA on 95th and Budlong Avenue. I watched a fifth-grade boy beat up my sister, Dee-Dee, right in our front yard. I screamed for him to stop. I called for help, but no one came. *Did I contribute to that?* I wondered. *What could I have done differently?* Hit him with a rock? Fight back? I froze. My screams were swallowed by the roar of a helicopter overhead while boys from school stood just outside our fence, watching. They couldn't step in—even when my mother wasn't home, no one was allowed past that gate. That boy was trespassing, and he was committing a crime.

When my mother got home from work that night, she was furious. The next day, my brothers found him and returned the favor. He never bothered my sister again, and the trauma of what I had seen stayed with me. I vowed never to let a boy or a man put his hands on me like that. Just ask George from College Park, GA—the boy I nearly drowned for trying to take off my bathing suit top.

As an adult, Dee-Dee found herself in another relationship—this time with a man who was physically abusive, even while she was pregnant with her second child. But this time, I didn't freeze. I grabbed a plumber's wrench and threatened to crack his skull open if he ever laid a hand on her again. He left, and I went straight to my sister to see if she was okay. She was grateful I was there. But later, she called our mother to come pick me up.

Dee-Dee wasn't emotionally strong then—not just because she was pregnant, but because no one had ever taught her what to do in a situation like this. My guess is, this wasn't the first time. Her light was undeniable. Her smile brightened the room the moment she walked in. She was a proud nerd, deeply passionate about learning with dreams of becoming a nurse. While working toward that goal, she also had to provide for her two sons. Her life was cut tragically short—far too soon, by our measure. Her sons were only one and two years old—too young to remember her. It is now up to me and my siblings to make sure her story is never forgotten.

For years, I dimmed my light to make others comfortable. Whether in church, school, the community, or the workplace, I was met with resistance the moment I walked in. My confidence was high, my spirit was joyful, and I genuinely loved people—I always have, even as a child. I was talkative then, and I still am now.

In many of my relationships, my personality was seen as *too much*. If I've had ten long-term relationships, nine of them were with men who felt I needed to *tone it down*. They told me I smiled too wide, showed too many teeth, or that my eyes sparkled just a little too much. They made me feel as if my light was a problem, so I dimmed it. I shrank myself so they could shine. I quieted my joy to avoid being misunderstood. I played small to sidestep accusations of being *too much*. I see it clearly now—it wasn't me. It was them, and yet, in a way, it *was* me. Because I allowed it. I wasn't just dimming my personality—I was dimming my purpose, my ministry, my calling. Never again.

Get this—I was feeling good about myself, about what God was doing in my life, and about the deep joy that comes from within. Then someone comes along and says, *"Hey, your light is too bright. It hurts my eyes."* And just like that, to keep the peace and avoid conflict, I started trimming myself down, and I mean *everything*. I toned down how I dressed. I changed the way I spoke to people—especially men. I even adjusted my voicemail message, making sure it wasn't *too* warm, *too* inviting. I muted the vibrant colors I loved—yellows, oranges, greens, reds—all because past relationships made me feel like I was *too much*. What I didn't realize then was that my light wasn't just *mine*—it came from Christ. It radiated from the inside out. And every time I dimmed that inner light, the rest of me faded too.

I've come to understand that it was never about me being *too much*—it was about others feeling *not enough.* My nephew once told me, *"Don't dim your light. Tell them to put on some sunglasses."* So, hear it from me first—if my light is too bright for you, either look away or put on some shades because I will never dim it again.

A Core Memory

When I was younger, I was full of life—always smiling, always laughing, always finding joy in the simplest moments. I loved people, loved connecting, sharing, and bonding. But somewhere between *then* and *now,* I lost sight of that. It happened slowly, almost without me realizing it. I entered a relationship where my partner's insecurities became the weight that dimmed my light.

A simple *good morning* or *hello*—especially to a man—would turn into an issue later, behind closed doors. I was accused of flirting. He would ask, *"Why do you smile so much? Why is your smile so bright? Why do you seem happier when certain people are around, but not when you're with me?"* Over time, those accusations took a toll on me. Years of walking on eggshells chipped away at who I was. And now, in my 50's, I find myself acting sheltered. I don't go many places alone. I've missed out on experiences, on moments, on *life* because I unknowingly carried the weight of that past. But here's the good part— **I found my light again.** For so long, I feared it might be too late to rediscover *me.* But slowly, I did. I found that little girl again—the giddy one who smiles and laughs at silly things, who enjoys dumb jokes and goofy movies. I missed her, and I think she missed me too.

They say a girl chooses a man just like her father. My biological father was barely present. Growing up, I saw him *maybe* once a year. And when I became an adult, our conversations were filled with blame. He accused my mother of putting a hex on him, called her vile names, and made her the scapegoat for all his misfortunes. In my mind, that wasn't a *curse*—it was *vengeance*, and vengeance belongs to God. Thankfully, I had a few positive father figures—my Uncle David, my pastors, and older teachers. But strangely enough, the one who had the greatest influence on me was the one who was never there.

I was told he had been abusive to my mother, cruel and unkind. Maybe that's why, as a teenager and into my early adult years, I found myself drawn to men who mistreated me. If that old adage is true, then I guess I did choose men like my father. And what kind of man was he? Like hot, human shrapnel—damaging everything he touched.

When my mother married Robert T. Johnson in 1997, he sealed the deal with me. At their reception, he stood up and said, *"Your kids are my kids, and your grandkids are my grandkids."* That was all I needed to hear. Truth be told, I had been acting a *plumb fool* leading up to their wedding. Why? Because just a few months before *their* big day, I had gotten engaged—and suddenly, I wasn't the center of attention.

Shameful, I know. But at the time, I was caught up in my feelings. Looking back, I can laugh at it now. In that moment, when Robert made that declaration, all of that pettiness melted away. I knew he was the real deal.

My Life, My Journey

Self-reflection has been the key to my growth and healing. I've witnessed firsthand how my own transformation has inspired others. I've also learned that true change isn't about quick fixes—it's about the long game. It's a lifelong journey, not a temporary shift. The pandemic forced me to take a hard look in the mirror and ask the tough questions. I prayed—*a lot*—asking God to reveal where I needed to grow, where I needed to show up differently, and how I needed to carry myself. As someone in leadership roles, I knew I had to be honest with myself. I had to evaluate not just my actions, but their impact. Through that process, I came up with a few questions that helped guide me—maybe they can help you, too:

1. How does my constant fussing, yelling, or saying *"because I said so"* affect those around me?
2. Do I have meaningful, effective communication with my friends, coworkers, and neighbors?
3. Why aren't people coming to me for guidance or support?
4. Why *are* people coming to me? Growth requires both reflection and change. If we're

going to evolve, we must do it together—honoring both their thoughts and my own.

5. Am I truly okay with not always being the one in charge?

Growth isn't just about looking inward—it's about moving forward with wisdom, humility, and grace. It took me about a year to answer question number five. And the answer? Yes. If something positive is happening, I'm all in—I don't need to be in charge. Now, let's talk about building relationships.

Over the past year, I made the decision to put myself out there and start dating again. And just like that, the first episode of my personal soap opera began—with a dating app. I've tried dating apps before, and let's just say I've been scammed a time or two. The pattern is almost laughably predictable:

The man is always a widower with one child—a child who's either a minor or conveniently studying medicine abroad. He himself works offshore or is some sort of engineer. And the conversation? Well, it always starts something like this:

Him: "Hi, Beautiful!"

Me: "Hello."

Him: "I love your pictures. You're such a pretty lady."

Me: "Thank you."

Then, right on cue, the questions start rolling in: *Are you married? Do you have children? Any daughters? How many? What are their ages?*

And the grand finale—*"Can we move this conversation off the app? I'm not on here much."* That is an Immediate red flag. If he can't address me by my *name* instead of "Beautiful," he's getting blocked.

A few more swipes, a few more conversations, and I found myself talking to men between the ages of 49 and 62. Out of five choices, four of them either talked way too much about nothing, were looking for a *bed warmer* (a.k.a. someone to casually sleep with), or had decided they were done with life and just wanted to "chill" after working 36 years at a job that drained the life out of them. But my *absolute favorites*? One man had **14 children** by **five different women** and was looking to *add more* to his legacy. The other was a man of very few words—except when it came to his never-ending list of medical issues. Every time I reached out, it was:

"Can we talk tomorrow? My gout is acting up today." Or *"I can't talk right now, my sciatica is flaring up."* I was like, "Sir. *You reached out to ME!*"

I decided to swipe again and came across a guy who seemed like a solid choice. His photo was nice, his profile checked a lot of boxes—he worked for the U.S. Postal Service, was an entrepreneur, and best of all, he was local. We started chatting here and there while we were both at work. He was a veteran, a martial arts instructor for kids on the weekends, and even a private driver for some famous folks (and yes, he sent pictures as *proof*). Our conversations, at least from my perspective, were going well. That is... until I accidentally mixed him up with another guy I had swiped on. And just like that, we never spoke again. That was the moment I decided *not* to juggle multiple conversations at once. From then on, I stuck to swiping on *one* person at a time and gave it a few days to see where things went— lesson learned.

My last swipe on the app was *a doozie*. Let's call him "J." He was 52-years-old, a driver, and he lived locally. We talked for about two weeks before deciding to meet in person. Since my oldest son and his family were in town, I let them know my plans. I told them I'd be meeting "J" at a local park and would be back before dark. Just to be safe, I shared his photo and my location with my son before heading out.

When I arrived, J looked just like his photo—a promising start. Our conversation flowed easily, and things seemed to be going well. Judging by the way he kept smiling and staring at me, I'd say he liked what he saw. A good sign... I guess. As the sun began to set, my son started calling me. Not wanting to be rude, I ignored my phone and kept chatting. When I finally got home, I casually shared my experience with my son and daughter-in-law, thinking everything had gone smoothly. My son, however, was *not* amused. My daughter-in-law smirked and said, *"Ms. Laura, he was about to come find you."* I laughed at first, but then I apologized for not answering my phone. *Is this what it feels like to have a parent watching over you?* Back in the day, I always made it home on time, so I never had the experience of being tracked down by worried family members. Looks like life has come full circle—except now, *I'm* the one being checked on.

I kept talking to J, and over the next few weeks, our interactions mostly consisted of phone calls and meetings at the park. Eventually, we started discussing going on an actual date to a restaurant. Before locking in any plans, I decided to call up an *old head* for some advice. His wisdom? Straight to the point. He said, *"All men are visual. There's nothing wrong with wanting to look sexy and smell good. But watch out for yellow flags—yellow means caution. If he's on a date with you and can't keep his eyes off other women, let him go. If he doesn't know how to hold a conversation and keep your attention, that's a yellow flag too."* Then came the best piece of advice: *"A man will always tell on himself—if you let him talk long enough."*

With that in mind, J and I tried to agree on a restaurant. That, surprisingly, turned into an issue. Not because I was picky, but because I had already been to most of the places he suggested. Not necessarily *with another man,* just that I was familiar with the menu and the prices. But I could tell "J" was not happy about that. *So what? We're not teenagers.*

Then came the next yellow flag. J kept commenting, *"These prices are high!"* To which I'd respond, *"We can go somewhere more within your budget. I'm not too picky."* As we kept discussing where to go, his conversation took a turn. Suddenly, he started complaining—about his bills, his paycheck being short, not being able to make deliveries like he used to, having to move out of his apartment... and a whole list of other *very* unattractive things. And just like that, the date I was once looking forward to started looking like a *huge* yellow flag waving right in front of me.

I gave it a couple more weeks, hopeful that something would change. It didn't. J continued talking—mostly about his finances. Then, out of nowhere, he started bringing up marriage, buying a house, and even leaving the state. He wanted me to sell *my* house and use the money to buy one for *us.* Oh, and he *really* didn't like that my children had keys to my house or that we were so close.

Through all his talking, I learned a few more things—none of them good. Turns out, he had three children he *wasn't* close with. He said they had a "falling out" years ago but admitted he hadn't made any effort to reconnect. On top of that, he had no stable housing and was *couch surfing.* At this point, the yellow flags had officially turned *red.*

Then came another moment that sealed the deal. J got sick at work and couldn't do his route. Wanting to be kind, I took him some ginger ale, napkins, and water. He was appreciative—at first. But later, he started hinting that he needed help paying his bills. That was my cue to exit stage left. I NEVER offered to give or loan him money. He's a grown man, and a grown man needs to handle his own business.

Oh, wait—I forgot something. Before J got sick, we had plenty of conversations about faith. He told me he accepted Christ while in the military, but oddly enough, he didn't own a Bible. Maybe he sensed I was picking up on some inconsistencies because, out of nowhere, he started asking if I wanted to have a private Bible study with him on Wednesdays—just the two of us. That was a *hard no*. I was already in a Bible study on Wednesdays.

Another conversation we had was about my stance on *not playing house*. J had a different perspective. He would often ask if I wanted to do a sexual *"test drive"* to make sure *everything* worked. His reasoning? *"What if we aren't compatible in bed? If we get married, we won't be happy."* My response? *"First of all, after a certain age, without a prescription, you probably wouldn't be able to do much in that department anyway. If we can't be friends now, how can we be friends later?"* And just to shut it down completely, I added, *"There's no need for a test drive. Mine works just fine."*

Two weeks later, I ended everything. Unfortunately, it was over the phone—but considering that's where most of our conversations took place anyway, it felt fitting. I took the easy route and told him, *"It's not you, it's me."* We hung up, and I exhaled. A week later, J sent me a text:

"I was just reaching out to say hello and see how you're doing. I probably won't reach out again because of the unknown. Take care."

My response? *"Okay."* One last thing—I forgot to mention that we kissed one time. Big mistake. I should *never* have done that. My kisses will make a man propose. I'm not even lying.

The question at the top of this chapter asks, *"What are you going to do about it?"* After this fiasco, my answer was simple—I deleted every dating app and decided to let God do what only He can do. If it's meant to be, it has to happen *organically.* I had already tried at least five different dating apps, and every single one led to the same outcome—*low-hanging fruit.* Enough was enough.

As the new year approached, my focus shifted entirely to *me.* I ate well, lost weight, and revamped my wardrobe. More importantly, I was happy and content—fully at peace with God and myself. If He decided to have the right man *find* me, great. If not, that was fine too. Someone on *Divorce Court* once said, *"You can't blame a clown for being a clown. Instead, ask yourself why you keep going to the circus."* Well, the circus had officially left town—also known as *I deleted the app.* Surely, the next one had to be better... right? And then—out of the blue—I met someone. I wasn't expecting it. I wasn't looking for it.

His name was Clifford. Tall, good-looking, well-read, educated, and resourceful. He said he was a Christian, though he had grown up attending a Catholic church. We started talking consistently for about a week after meeting through a mutual friend. He had never been married but said he had *come close.* He also had no children—not by circumstance, but by choice. He had decided long ago that he wouldn't have kids until he was married. A noble stance, right? He also stated that he planned to remain celibate until marriage—and I agreed.

At first, he seemed to be checking a lot of boxes. He wasn't a smoker. He was self-employed. He had a good head on his shoulders. Without giving away too much about him, I will say this—some of my friends and family met him, and they got along well. He had even been to my home— something I *never* allow—and we had gone on two dates prior. Things seemed to be going in the right direction. *Seemed.*

After six weeks of talking, Clifford mentioned that he had spoken to a longtime friend about me after our dates—and apparently, his friend really liked me just from what he'd heard. That alone wasn't a big deal. But what *did* catch my attention was when Clifford casually mentioned that on our *very first date*, while we were riding in the car to our location, he had actually called this friend so we could talk. *That* perked up my ears. Then, later in the conversation, he dropped this gem: *"I told him I'm not dating. I'm vetting Laura right now."* My face immediately twisted up. If you've read any of my other books, you *already* know what that means. I looked at him and said, *"I'm not applying for a job. Who else are you 'vetting'? I don't spend time like this with people who are in an interview process."* Now, in all fairness, he's from New York, and maybe that's just the language they use in his neighborhood. He didn't like my tone, and I didn't care.

The remainder of our time together felt uncertain. We still talked on the phone, but our conversations became shallow. I found myself *forcing* topics just to keep the dialogue going. During one of those conversations—while Clifford was at my home—I asked him, *"What do you think it takes to get and keep a woman like me?"* His response? *"I need to step it up! I need to step up my game!"* I told him he was absolutely right. And I also made it clear—I was *not* going to compromise where I stood.

Physically, our relationship had very little intimacy. We never kissed and *barely* held hands. For the most part, he was a gentleman—he opened doors, pulled out chairs, walked on the street side, and always came to my door to pick me up. He even made sure I was securely in the car before closing the door. Women *love* that. But here's the thing—*chivalry alone isn't enough.*

71

What he *wasn't* doing was showing that he could bring more to the table than just words and witty conversation. And that was a problem.

One day, I got a text from Clifford. He wanted to take me somewhere and show me something. I already had plans with my family that day, but he assured me I wouldn't be late for my event, so I agreed. He drove me to a house in a *very* prominent neighborhood. Confused, I asked, *"Why are we here?"* His response? *"I want to build with you. I find myself being pulled in by your beauty."* I was *not* impressed.

First off, the house was nearly *two million dollars, tiny*, and *not* worth the price. And while we were standing there, Clifford tried to show me a bank receipt from a recent deposit—like that was supposed to impress me. I waved it off. I didn't need to see it. That money could have belonged to *anybody.* I wasn't interested in his bank balance. I wanted to know what was in his *heart.* Then, out of nowhere, he hit me with:

"Can we test drive in the bedroom to see if we're compatible?" Are you hearing the theme song from the *last* episode? Because I sure was.

At this point, it was clear—this man was trying to impress me with:

✔ Money he didn't have

✔ A house he couldn't afford

✓ And empty words

And here's the kicker—I had *no* idea if he was actually a millionaire or not. What I *did* know was that he had *nothing* to show for it. When I asked to see where he lived (*since he rented a room*), he pulled out pictures...Of his *old* apartment. In *New York.* Yeah. You already know how this ended.

I shared more with Clifford than I had with any of the *circus clowns* before him. I even told him about how I had been ghosted in 2016 by a man I truly thought I would marry. Clifford's response? *"I'll never ghost you because I know how that feels."* Fast forward to month three of our *talking, vetting,* or whatever you want to call it—and things were unraveling fast. Turns out, Clifford was *also* vetting another woman.

Because I've lived in this community for a long time, and people knew we were dating, I started getting reports—eyewitness accounts of him out and about with someone else. When I asked him about it, he denied everything. *Of course, he did.* At that moment, I made a choice—to *get out of God's way.* From the start, I had prayed for clarity, asking God to reveal what I needed to see about Clifford. But now? I was getting *real* persistent. I wasn't about to waste more precious time on something that wasn't aligned with God's will.

April 5, 2024, was the last time we exchanged calls or texts. Then, on April 8, 2024, I got a message—from *the other woman.* She couldn't find Clifford. He wasn't responding to her calls or texts. I kept it simple: *"I'm sure he's fine. He's a grown man. He'll turn up."* But she wasn't buying it. Instead, she sent me pictures of his car—license plate, make, model, *last known whereabouts.* And all I could think was, *This is odd. I don't even have my kids' information like this.*

She told me they had been together on the night of April 5th—the *same* night Clifford and I last spoke—and that he had wanted to spend the night *again.* Now, I'll admit, my response was a little messy: *"Oh? And why exactly would he be spending the night?"* When Clifford finally resurfaced, he went exactly where he *wanted* to be—with her. I wasn't mad—I hadn't invested much in the relationship. But I *was* disappointed. I had at least expected him to be man enough to tell me he wasn't interested in that way. As B. Sankey once said, *"If I'm not a choice, I'm definitely not an option."*

I shared this experience with a male friend, and he didn't hold back. He said, *"A Black man his age who has never been married and has no children is usually one of three things—gay, a playboy, or dealing with mental health issues."* He also believed that Clifford probably didn't expect to *actually* like me—so he ran.

Through all this so-called *vetting,* I had learned something crucial about Clifford: he was a man who *needed* constant praise. He thrived on validation, needed to be patted on the back, spoken about in admiration, and to be loved to the *last drop*. Now, I wouldn't have minded that—if he wasn't also seeking it from other women. But here's the thing: by the time I met Clifford, I had *grown*. I had *healed*. I wasn't *thirsty*. And Clifford? He *needed* a thirsty woman. Someone who would not only feed his ego but also *fund his lifestyle*. For all his education, prospects, connections, and intellect, he was still *acting* and *living* like *low-hanging fruit*. And the crazy part is, he wasn't even on an app.

What I Decided to Do

I prayed for him. Not just for Clifford, but for myself—that if I ever saw him again, I wouldn't feel any animosity toward him. I remember when I craved validation so badly that *not* receiving it felt crippling. I know what it's like to want genuine love but be rejected in my truth. That's why I couldn't be mad. Disappointed? Yes. But bitter? No. One of my sons saw Clifford twice and asked if I wanted him to say something to him about how we left things. My answer was always the same: *"No. He's not worth it."*

I've run into him a handful of times since, and we don't speak. He doesn't acknowledge me, and I don't acknowledge him. And honestly, what would we even say?

"Hey! You ghosted me!"

"Hey! Sorry I was juggling another woman while talking to you!" No thanks.

I had already gotten *everything* I needed to move forward. And I was more than content with myself. In fact, I saw it as a setup—if Clifford got the chance to meet some of my friends and family, then surely, this was just a preview for the *real MVP...* the one *who actually belongs here.*

Lessons to Remember When People Reject You

1. **It's not worth the jail time**.
2. **It's not you who they're rejecting—it's what you carry that they can't handle**. The best way for them to admit that? By walking away like the coward they are. Don't be bitter. Judge Lynn Toler once said, *"Bitterness allows the offender to hurt you every day anew."*
3. **Follow God's way, not your own**. James 1:22-24 reminds us that anyone who reads Scripture but doesn't follow God's way is only deceiving themselves. If I had gone my own way, my sons would have gotten involved.
4. **Hurt people, hurt people**.
5. **Pastor Steven Furtick said**, *"You might have to move forward into this season of your life without preparation, and you might have to figure it out as you go."* Keep going anyway.
6. **"When God shows you something about someone, don't dismiss it. It's clarity you prayed for, not confusion."** — Faith.Factor.Media
7. **Attraction does not equal God's approval**. 2 Corinthians 6:14 reminds us:

"Do not be unequally yoked with unbelievers. For what fellowship hath righteousness with unrighteousness? And what communion hath light with darkness?" Bottom line? I had *no business* with Clifford in the first place—not even as a friend.

8. **Are you arrogant or confident?** Do you know the difference?

At the beginning of this chapter, I asked myself, *What am I gonna do about it?* I prayed. God showed me the warning signs—over and over. But like so many women, I rationalized them away... until the trash started stinking so bad, I couldn't ignore it anymore. Once I realized what was *stinkin'*, it was over. And guess what? He walked away before I could—*which worked out even better for me.*

Chapter Five

S.E.X. Change

Pay Attention as You Panic, or You'll Have Problems

For most of my life, I thought I had grown up eating off a silver spoon—because I never went without. Turns out, that spoon was *plastic*. But still, I *never* missed a meal. So much of what we saw on TV growing up focused on physical fitness—exercise routines, diet plans, and how to stay in shape. But as I mentioned in another chapter, rarely did anyone talk about *self-improvement* or **Self-EXamination** from the inside out. And if there's one thing I've learned, it's this: **Life is not a sprint—it's a marathon.**

In my lifetime, I've participated in and completed *seven* Los Angeles Marathons. Two of them were the bike marathon. The cycling course was 24 miles; the running course, a grueling 26.2 miles. And let me tell you—every non-professional runner will say the same thing: it's the last **.2 miles** that'll break you. Of course, running takes longer, but riding a bike for that distance comes with its own dangers. Just like the runners, spectators line up to cheer on the cyclists. The difference? In a running marathon, if someone steps on the back of your foot, your shoe might come off. In a *bike* marathon, if someone clips your back tire, you're *going down*—and you're probably taking 20 or more riders down with you. The first time I saw that many people crash, I was *traumatized.* I prayed right then and there, *Lord, please don't let that be me.*

Learning to Pace Myself

My first running marathon was *brutal.* Well—honestly, they *all* were. But after my first few, I learned something critical: **Don't panic in the crowd.** Picture this—the excitement the day before race day. Going to the L.A. Convention Center to pick up my goodie bag, my timing chip, and, of course, taking those *fake* finish-line photos like I had already conquered the race. The atmosphere was electric. I was *hyped* knowing I was one of 40,000 people who had registered.

Then, there were the bib numbers. Mine? Somewhere in the *tens of thousands.* The elite runners? Their bibs were single or double digits. And let's be honest—that number placement almost determines where you'll finish... or if you'll even *finish* at all.

The Breaking Point

For the first nine miles, I was *flying.* Holding a steady **7-to-10-minute mile** pace. The streets were lined with friendly faces, cheering us on. Rock bands played on every other block, keeping the energy high and making me feel like I was an *Olympian.* No one warned me that, eventually, the crowd would thin out. See, half of those runners were only in it for the **5K** or **10K**. That meant *we,* the *crazy ones* pushing for the full **26.2 miles**, were about to hit the hardest part of the race *alone.* Then it happened.

I could feel my body getting *heavy.* Lactic acid settled in my thighs like cement. And then, the humbling moment—old men, twice my age, were passing me *with ease.* Steady, strong, disciplined. Meanwhile, I was struggling. By mile **14**, I gave in. I decided to stop and walk. That was a big mistake. My *mind* was screaming at me to stop, but my *legs* weren't on board. They still wanted to run. I tried to start again, but now my whole body was fighting itself. I must have looked *ridiculous*—like I was trying to kick-start a human stick shift. It was horrible. And then? **I panicked.** I thought, *"My car is too far away. How am I supposed to get home if I stop now?"* I was *tired.* I was *scared.* I felt *stuck.* So, I did the only thing I knew to do. I **prayed.** *"God, I need help. I don't know if I can do this. Please, send help now!"* And **He did.**

God Always Sends Who You Need

Just as I was about to break down completely, a woman named **Gabrielle** appeared beside me. She was tired too. We started talking—about kids, life, friendships, and things I can't even remember now. But what I *do* remember is that she said something that changed everything: *"I'll stay with you until the end."* I looked at her and smiled. *"I just prayed, and God answered."*

We ran a little, walked a little, and talked the whole time. At one point, we even tried speed-walking—but that backfired *quickly.* By then, I had started calling her *Gaby.* She turned to me and said, *"We're gonna finish these last two-point-two miles running."* I nodded. *Agreed.* And when the time came, we jogged as best as we could. Crossing that finish line together, we threw our hands up in victory! Somewhere, tucked away in my storage boxes, there's a picture of that moment—a reminder of a race I almost didn't finish, and the stranger who wouldn't let me quit.

We got our aluminum foil blankets, our post-race snacks, took pictures with our medals, exchanged emails, hugged, and said our goodbyes. I was *so* grateful to God for sending her my way. I had been *ready* to give up. But He heard my cry. Gaby and I kept in touch for about a month. And then—she was gone. I never saw or heard from her again. I tried emailing her once, but it bounced back with *"undeliverable."* That's when it hit me. God had sent me exactly what I needed, exactly *when* I needed it. An angel, named **Gabrielle**. (*Gabriel.*)

A Few Questions to Ponder:

1. Are you a strong support or resource for others? If not, why?
2. Can you point people in the right direction when they need guidance?
3. Will you partner with someone to ensure their success?
4. What does fellowship look like to you?
5. Pay close attention to the relationships you engage in and the people you attach yourself to. **Ask yourself—why?**

Never underestimate the power of the top sheet mindset.

I remember seeing a debate on social media about whether the top sheet in a sheet set was *necessary*. The opinions were split 50/50. The *old-school* crowd swore by it, calling it a *safety net*—a barrier between the blanket and the fitted sheet. Others dismissed it as unnecessary, saying it just got in the way. But here's the thing—the **top sheet serves a purpose.** It creates a **protective layer** between you and a rough, prickly blanket or an itchy wool comforter. It also helps keep your blanket and comforter clean longer.

In a way, having a top sheet mindset is a lot like how God sent me Gaby. It keeps you from giving up, reminding you that you're protected. It acts as a barrier—standing between you and whatever is trying to wear you down. I know people who sleep on the top sheet but never get under it. Their reasoning? They don't want the extra effort of making up their beds in the morning. But if they really understood its purpose *what a difference that would make!*

Learning to Trust the Climb

In 2005, I had the opportunity to chaperone a youth retreat in the mountains. One of the trust exercises was called *Climbing the Wall.* Now, in theory, it sounded simple. I was harnessed in, securely tethered to someone below, which meant I *couldn't* fall. But knowing that didn't stop me from being *terrified.* With a lot of encouragement, I kept climbing—higher and higher. Then, at some point, **I froze.** Panic took over, and I found myself stuck—arms and legs splayed out like a *chalk outline at a crime scene.* I felt *trapped.*

Going up felt impossible. Going down felt like *defeat.* My heart was racing. I wasn't crying, but I was *this close.* Eventually, the instructor had to come up and rescue me. And after that? I *vowed* never to do it again. Looking back, my real problem wasn't the wall—it was *trust.* I didn't trust my instructor. I didn't trust the harness. I let fear paralyze me.

Isn't that exactly how we treat God sometimes?

We make big, bold decisions. We start climbing. We tell ourselves, *I got this!* Then, somewhere along the way, we get stuck. We panic. And instead of trusting Him, we freeze.

The Comeback Climb

More than **ten years later**, I tried climbing the wall *again*. This time? I crushed it. I was scaling that thing like *Spider-Man*. The fear that once held me back was *gone*. I had *matured*, I had *healed*, and I had finally learned to *trust*. Sometimes, I wonder if God ever shakes His head at us when we get ourselves stuck and think, *"I'm not tryna save you from something you won't take care of."* In the end, **all I had to do was stay calm and trust.**

Questions to Ask Yourself:

1. What fear (or fears) are holding you back? *Why?*
2. Is it *really* fear, or have you just adopted a fearful mindset about new things?
3. What steps can you take to start overcoming it?
4. Who or what does your next move involve?
5. Do you have a plan, or are you just winging it?

6. Do you feel stuck?
7. What **adjustments** do you need to make to get back on course?

Take your time answering these questions in your own way—but be honest with yourself. True healing and growth can only happen when you're willing to face the truth.

When I was younger and still living at home, there were things my mother did—or told me to do— that never came with an explanation. Now, to be fair, we were raised *not* to ask why. But there were two things that puzzled me so much, I couldn't help myself. The first was her habit of opening a carton of eggs at the store *before* buying them. It seemed unnecessary, and she never explained why she did it.

The second was her insistence on shaking out wet towels—or any wet laundry—*before* putting them in the dryer. Again, no explanation. Just *do it*. It wasn't until *recently* that the lightbulb finally went on for both. With the towels, it was about airflow—shaking them out allows the heat to circulate better, ensuring they dry evenly. Otherwise, they'd feel dry on the outside but still be damp on the inside. And the eggs? Well, she was checking for cracks. Simple. Obvious. But to my younger self, it was just one of those *mom things* that made no sense at the time.

Then, in the last few months, another realization hit me—I was raised by a woman from the *Silent Generation*. And *that* explained a lot. Looking back, it makes sense why certain conversations never happened in our home. We never openly discussed **sex, politics, money, dating, marriage, Black history, Juneteenth, religion**—and so much more. My mother and her siblings were raised by men and women from the **Greatest Generation**, and in turn, they passed down that same *silent* approach to their children. And so, I was raised in a world where asking *why* wasn't just discouraged—it simply wasn't done.

When I was eight years old, my mother was dating a man who was *handsome* and *generous with his money*. He seemed genuinely interested in her, and he was loving towards me and my siblings as well. While visiting, he would often tinker with his car, calling me over to find random things—a **safety pin, an ink pen, a bobby pin, a hanger**, or whatever other odd item he could think of. Each time I brought him something, he handed me a dollar. Sometimes, he didn't even ask for anything. He would just call my name, reach into his pocket, and give me money.

One day, when it was just my mother and me, I asked her why he did that—why he gave me money even when I didn't ask for it. Her response was simple: *"Never question when someone gives you a gift. Just take it and be grateful."* At the time, I accepted her answer. But as I got older, I started to wonder *where* that belief came from. I imagine it was something she was told—maybe by *her* parents, or maybe by a man who once had power over her. Later in life, I learned that my mother had been in an abusive first marriage. And being raised in the *Silent Generation,* where difficult conversations were often avoided, it made sense why she would say something like that. Her words weren't just about *gratitude*—they were about **survival**.

I wish my mother and I had talked about her abusive relationships. Maybe it would have kept me from getting into my own. Or at the very least, when I *did* find myself in one, I might have spoken up instead of hiding it—from her, from my loved ones, from everyone who cared about me. There's something to be said about men and women who grow up witnessing abuse—whether it happens *to* them or to a parent figure. The damage doesn't just disappear. It lingers. It shapes us. And while healing *is* possible, the scars never fully fade. Sometimes, all it takes is a *word*, a *phrase*, a *song*, or even a *scent*—and suddenly, we're back there again, in the moment where it all began.

Pay Attention and Don't Panic

When I was nine years old, my mother enrolled us in swimming lessons. Her reasoning was simple: *"I never learned how to swim, and if one of y'all falls in, I can't save you."* At the time, we were living in Los Angeles, California, and we often walked to **Sportsman Pool** at the local Recreation Center for our lessons. I started as a **guppy**, swimming safely in the 3-foot deep section of the pool. But as I progressed to the next level—**goldfish**—it meant stepping (or rather, swimming) into deeper waters: the **5-foot**

section. The test? Swim freestyle to the other side of the pool, then swim *backward* on the way back.

At first, I kicked my legs and moved steadily through the water. But midway back, exhaustion hit. I stopped kicking and tried to float the rest of the way. That worked—*for a moment*. But soon, I realized I had completely stopped moving. And then? I just... gave up. I let myself **sink**. I could barely touch the bottom of the pool, balancing on the tips of my toes, but the water was still **over my head**. Holding my breath, I thought: *"Is this how I'm going to die?"* I wasn't afraid at the time. It was so peaceful under water. A lifeguard pulled me out, and my instructor immediately laid into me for stopping. I sat quietly by the poolside, too drained to argue. Even now, when I think back to that moment, the only explanation I have for why I stopped is **I was tired**. Simple, yet profound. But here's what I know now—**God had a plan for my life.**

Do You Ever Wonder...

- *God, I don't know what Your plan is, but I'm tired.*
- *Why didn't I die?*
- *What if I had died? How would it have affected the people around me?*

That day, my **fight or flight** response was *absent*. I chose neither. I simply gave in. And I've learned the hard way—people like me are not allowed to just *be tired* and give up. We have to **keep going**—for ourselves, *and* for the people who depend on us. Oh, and by the way? I'm a *great* swimmer now.

Chapter Six

Smoke Breaks

Food for Thought | Words of Encouragement

When I was a little girl, my mother smoked cigarettes—indoors, outdoors, wherever she needed to. This was long before the Surgeon General started warning people about the dangers of secondhand smoke. I remember waking up in the middle of the night and seeing a small glowing light in the corner of the room. At first, I didn't think much of it. But when the light shifted slightly, I realized—it was my mother, cigarette in hand, watching over us as we slept.

Now that I understand how hard it was for her—**a single mother of nine children**—I can only imagine the thoughts running through her mind in those quiet moments. Maybe she was worrying about our safety, guarding us from the *real* boogeyman. Maybe she was thinking about where we would live in the next six months, knowing that staying at Grandma's was no longer an option and that our move to Georgia was coming soon. And maybe—just maybe—though she held a cigarette in one hand, she was **holding a prayer in the other**.

My grandmother was *fierce*! She never learned to drive, but she **worked hard, played hard, prayed hard**—and let me tell you, she **whooped hard too** (only once on me, but that was *enough*). She had *zero* tolerance for sass or backtalk—especially from a boy. She said what she meant and meant what she said. One evening, she told me to come inside and take my bath before dark. I ignored her. When I finally strolled into the back room, there she was—waiting. Before I could react, she snatched me up. I tried to crawl away on my knees, but she had already locked my head *between* her knees and she **tore my butt up!** I *swear* I saw fireworks that night—and every single one was coming from her *hits*.

She didn't just discipline—she *enforced*. Like the time she told my brother *not* to play his tuba in the house. He didn't listen. He kept doing it. So, one day, while he was at school, I watched as she calmly picked up that tuba... took it outside... and **set it on fire. Yes, on fire.** My brother had to explain to his band director what happened. But here's the best part—**the director didn't even argue.** He understood something unspoken but *universal*: **When a Black grandmother gives a directive, you listen.** If you *don't*, you *deal* with the consequences.

My mother was a *beast* of a woman—not in a mean way, but in a **stern, no-nonsense, handle-**

her-business kind of way. She didn't tolerate much foolishness from us, and she *definitely* didn't believe in sparing the rod. Yet, despite her toughness, we never went without. We were *spoiled*—not with excess, but with **everything we needed** and even some of what we *wanted*. She lived in "Beast Mode" for most of my life, always working hard to provide for us. Growing up, I learned that sometimes, life means *waiting your turn*. And looking back, I realize my mother spent most of her years putting **us** first, rarely doing anything for herself. As the youngest of **nine** children, I know there was plenty I missed out on. But in our house, **kids weren't allowed in grown folks' business**—so whatever I *didn't* see, I wasn't meant to see.

My stepfather was a **gentle soldier**—a man of quiet strength and unwavering principles. Though he only had an eighth-grade education, he was incredibly intelligent. He had a sharp mind, a deep sense of discipline, and financial wisdom that many people with degrees never master. He **paid cash for everything**. The only credit card he owned was strictly for emergencies.

One of his favorite things to do was eat at a local restaurant with me. He loved **God**, and he was deeply committed to organizations that uplifted Black communities. At church, he served as an usher, and for more than **65 years**, he remained a faithful member of the **Automobile Club of California**. I remember looking at his membership card and thinking, *"Dang! That's a long time to be faithful to something."* He also had a way of keeping my grammar sharp. On multiple occasions, he corrected my grammar. Once, I asked, *"Where are you at?"* Without missing a beat, he said, *"Putting 'at' at the end of a question is inappropriate. It's a preposition, and you don't end a sentence with a preposition."* Not bad for a man who left school after middle school to explore the world. I've tried to correct myself when speaking. *Texting, though? That's a different story.*

Are you the kind of person who hates missing out? Ever find yourself holding it in just so you don't miss a moment of your favorite show—even when you really need a bathroom break? That's what **commercials** are for. The same goes for life. Sometimes, we get so caught up in what's happening that we forget to pause, breathe, and reflect. These moments are your *commercial break*—your chance to reset before moving forward.

More Food for Thought & Encouragement:

- Not everyone will read about you, see you, or feel the impact of your contribution. **That's why you do what you can today and leave the rest to history.**
- *White-knuckled faith* is what will take you to the next level. **Do it bold. Do it scared. Do it right—or don't do it at all.** I've seen people do things just for shock value. But is it because they don't feel *valued*? People may remember the act, but **will they remember their character?**

- Ever caught yourself thinking, *"I wish God would stick to the script"*? But *what script?* **He wrote it, not us.** And if we had written it, it would be a disaster for sure.
- My big sister Dee-Dee was murdered in 1987. It took me nearly 30 years to forgive the man who took her life.
- As I've gotten older, I still have the same fire—I just rely on a **different heat source**.
- No matter how much our kids mess up in *our* eyes, they are **always redeemable in God's eyes**.
- *Mental health* = a **healthy mentality for healing**.
- People will often try to **discourage you**— just like the crowd did to **Blind Bartimaeus. Keep calling out. Jesus hears you.**
- Disciplining a child with a **learning disability** for using their own mind is *ludicrous.* They're not rebellious; they're *processing* differently. **Guide them—don't punish them for thinking.**
- All my life, I've tried to **trick God**—and guess what? It *doesn't* work.
- Don't be surprised when people take advantage of **extended grace**.
- **A moment of transparency:** I used to wait for a man to *rescue* me—not realizing **THE Man** had already saved me. My mistake? **I kept going back to situations that required continuous rescuing.** Don't do that.

- Some people just need to admit **they were wrong** and ask for forgiveness. *We already know.*
- **I'm not looking for a man, but I'm accepting applications.** Don't come at me with the *"God sent me"* line unless **He prepared me, too.** If God is behind it, **both will be sent, and both will be ready.**
- **Oprah Winfrey** said, *"People don't always like you. They're not always happy for you. And if you surround yourself with people who are not accustomed to your success, they become fearful because you're reflecting something they don't recognize."*
- Generations are **scattered** because souls are **torn and tattered**—bound by secrets, lies, and ties that need to be broken. **Healing starts when you stop losing pieces of yourself just to keep the peace.**
- Sometimes, being **single** feels like being the *dish at the potluck that nobody really wants to eat.* People pick up the spoon, smell it, frown, and move on to something that looks *familiar*—something they *think* will taste better.
- Did you know most people don't like the **"butt bread"** of the loaf? But that piece **protects the middle** from going stale. *Oh, how I have served as the butt bread to so many...*
- You can't be a **silo** and expect things to change. **People help us grow. People force us to grow. Stay connected.**
- **Pastor Keion Henderson** said, *"We must be strategic in how we move. Patience is a*

strategy." **Isaiah 30: "They that wait on the Lord shall renew their strength."**

- Two years ago, a single male friend and I made a *pact*—if neither of us was married in a year, we'd marry each other. **He broke the pact. He's married now.** I should've gotten it *in writing...* and *notarized.*
- *Rich people get roaches too*—**the classy kind**. The ones that wait until guests leave before coming out. **Because they have manners.**
- **Chuck Swindoll** said, *"Contentment keeps you from being in competition."*
- Be careful about taking advice from people who say, *"You need to... you should... if I were you..."* unless they've actually done it *themselves.*
- Being in the **minority** doesn't shake you when you have **perspective** and **purpose**.
- **Don't count me in the number until my number gets called.**
- **I don't look like everybody else because I'm not everybody else.** *Duplication is prohibited.*
- *Why fight for something that's already mine?* **Because I don't realize it's mine.**
- *Why fight with someone who refuses to change?*
- Weak people need **backup**—they don't have the strength to **stand against the enemy** on their own.
- **They'll try to take my territory, but they won't get it. My name is on it.**
- **Everything that relies on you, the enemy will come after.**

- *Some men look. Some men glance. Some men glare. Some men stare.* Know the difference.
- *Sometimes, I just need 8 minutes.*
- **"Blood makes us related. Love makes us family."** – Michael Wilson, Jr.
- You must **shed old skin** to grow.
- **Ownership makes you unstoppable.**
- "**We are connected to everything but attached to nothing.**" – MWJ
- "**When we over-serve, we teach people NOT to love us.**" – Armon Patrick
- My new word is "**Comfortunate**"—which means one has *unfortunately conformed.*
- When you're *not* healthy within, you can't recognize **healthy relationships** in front of you.
- **Expectations are ultimatums. Boundaries are lines people will try to cross.** – MWJ
- *I despise pet names like honey, sugar, love, and dear.* **They are trigger words for me.**
- Don't aim to be a **third wheel**—aim to be a **second cousin**. Trying to force yourself into a relationship dynamic that doesn't fit? **That's ill-advised.** Be the first to say, **"I want better for myself"**—then **go get it.**

A third wheel is good for three things:

- ✓ **Trailers**

- ✓ **Tricycles**

- ✓ **Diffusing arguments**

Otherwise? Let it go.

Chapter Seven
A Slow Drag

Things to Ponder | Random Thoughts

We have become careless with other people's feelings—**because we don't have control over our own.** The filters we once relied on are full of holes, allowing everything slip through—unchecked, unfiltered, and unguarded. And as a result, we create **waves of insecurity**, expose **deep vulnerabilities**, and **crush** the very people we claim to care about.

Winning is no longer enough. Now, we chase the title of **ultimate winner**—but *why*? Is it because we want to be **placed above others**—so high that no one can reach us? So far removed that no one can touch us? Somewhere along the way, we stopped caring—not just about others, but about *ourselves*. And that **disconnect** is spreading like a disease, plaguing our communities. It is breeding a generation that is trapped between **entitlement and emptiness**—walking with a confidence they didn't earn, carrying a **disposition that could destroy them.** If we don't recognize the damage, how can we begin to heal?

By now, many of you have probably seen the movie *Sleeping With the Enemy*, based on the novel by Nancy Price, published in 1987. The story follows a young wife trapped in a marriage with a man who embodies **narcissistic abuse**— mentally and physically controlling, manipulative, blame-shifting, and distrustful of anyone outside their relationship. He threatens to kill her if she ever tries to leave, making escape seem impossible.

But here's what I want to share—**the enemy isn't always a person.** Everyone lives by a certain **lifestyle, belief system, or personal code**, whether they follow Christianity, another faith, or a completely different philosophy. Many religious paths have **mandates, rituals, and behaviors** that shape how people live. But the *real* enemy? It's **anything** or **anyone** that seeks to control, abuse, or manipulate you. It's the **gossip** you absorb throughout the day. It's the **mindless social media scrolling** that clutters your thoughts right before bed.

All of it—every toxic word, every piece of negativity—**finds rest in your mind** as you try to sleep. It infiltrates your subconscious, twisting into strange dreams, anxieties, and restless nights. **That** is sleeping with the enemy. Don't take those thoughts, those people, or that energy to bed with you. **Don't let it stunt your growth.**

Don't let it control you. At the end of the day, we all have a choice in **who and what we allow into our space—even in our sleep.**

What about the couple where one is **too gullible and vulnerable**, while the other is **manipulative and emotionally unstable**? That combination is a ticking time bomb. When one partner is too trusting and the other thrives on control, neither can function in a healthy way. **Communication suffers. Boundaries blur. Emotional stability crumbles.** Over time, the relationship **deteriorates**, leaving both people broken—each blaming the other for its downfall. This is yet another area where we can strive for change.

A healthier, more balanced life starts with **intentional choices**—even something as simple as getting **good sleep**. When we sleep well, we wake up **refreshed**. When we wake up refreshed, we have a **better day**. And when we have a better day, we're **more productive, more present, and more in control of our emotions**. The domino effect is powerful—but **it starts with small, intentional changes.**

The Church Is a Hospital

As a child, I learned that the **church is a hospital**—and every one of us is in a different department, seeking treatment for something. Some are in the **Emergency Room**, in crisis and desperate for immediate intervention.

Some are in **Urgent Care**, needing attention but not quite at the breaking point. Some are in **Triage**, trying to assess the severity of their wounds. Some are in the **Mental Health Ward**, battling unseen struggles. Some need **MRIs and X-rays**, searching for clarity on what's broken inside. Some are **bleeding out**, barely holding on.

Some require **chemo or radiation**, undergoing treatment for something toxic that's been growing within them for years. Some are **losing their eyesight**, unable to see what's right in front of them. Some are **struggling to hear**, missing the messages they need the most. Some are **holding onto the wall, trying to walk**, unsteady but still moving forward. Some are on the **roof, waiting to be airlifted**, hoping for a *miraculous* life-saving procedure.

Some need a **transplant**, requiring a total heart change. And then there are those who remain in the hospital **not because they want healing, but because they don't want to go home and face what's waiting for them.** Some stay because they like being served—pushing a button and expecting someone to respond. But healing isn't just about being treated, it's about **choosing to recover, to walk out of the hospital, and to live.**

Some treat others like expired food—quick to throw them away the moment they reach their so-called "Best By" date. *"If you're not who I want you to be by now, I'm walking away."* Or *"If your behavior doesn't change by this point, I'm done."* Just because someone hasn't *arrived* by a certain timeline doesn't mean they're no good. It simply means they're **in progress**—not where they *used* to be, but not quite where they *want* to be yet. **Growth takes time. Change takes time.** And real transformation doesn't come with an expiration date.

Have you ever been driving to work or a familiar location, taking the same route you always do? You know the road so well that you anticipate every turn, every stoplight—and even the dips in the pavement. What happens when you brace for a dip that **doesn't** happen? That happened to me one morning on my way to work. I tensed up, expecting the usual drop in the road—but when it didn't come, it **completely threw me off**. My stomach felt like it was dropping *anyway*, and for a split second, I didn't know how to react. Funny how something so small can shake you—simply because you were expecting one thing and got another.

Each time I've spoken at **breast cancer awareness events**, there has *always* been a Christian woman in the audience. I don't see that as coincidence—I see it as a **divine appointment**. For the woman who is already a believer, my words about faith serve as **encouragement**. For the woman who doesn't yet know Christ, I am there to **plant the seed**. And for the woman who is *teetering*—unsure, questioning, searching—**I may be the final push she needs**. God places us exactly where we need to be, and in those moments, I know **I am walking in purpose.**

There have been countless times when I've **delayed my own progress** by being disobedient. Sometimes, it was as simple as **entertaining the wrong conversations**—talking to someone I had no business talking to about things that **held no real value** and did nothing to move my life forward. Other times, it looked like **taking a job I had no business taking**—chasing money and titles instead of purpose. In one of those situations, I later realized I could have been **seriously hurt or even killed**—a reality that would have shattered my mother's heart.

There have been moments where I've taken **wrong turns for all the *right* reasons**—decisions that made logical sense at the time but ultimately cost me more than I knew. I may never fully know what I *missed out on*, but what I *do* know is this: **I don't want to miss out on anything else.** God has allowed me to catch glimpses of some of the opportunities I let slip away—some of them deeply important to me. But at the end of the day, **that was on me.** One of the hardest things I had to do was —**forgive myself, move forward, and refuse to make the same mistake again.** At the root of every setback is pride, blame, and unforgiveness. None of these build, they only tear down.

Throughout my life, I've been blessed with what some call **"spiritual fathers."** Two of the most influential were my Uncle David Russell and my former pastor. Both men played a huge role in my upbringing and spiritual development—guiding me from childhood, through my youth and young adulthood, and now into my **seasoned** years. Whenever I made a mistake, they didn't hesitate to call me out on it. Their words were enough to make me stop immediately. **I respected their authority and their wisdom.**

One memory, in particular, still stands out to this day. As a kid, I would often play with my former pastor's daughter, and we had a bad habit of running in and out of their house—slamming the screen door every single time. His wife would **yell at us** to stop, but like most kids, we didn't listen. We just kept doing it. For **thirty minutes straight**, we ran back and forth—until suddenly, on one of our trips through the door, **we stopped dead in our tracks.** Standing there, blocking the doorway, was **my pastor.** All I could see was **a tall, dark shadowy figure**, the gleam of **gold buttons on his three-piece suit**, and the shimmer of **jewelry catching the light.** We didn't need a sermon. We didn't need a word. **We just knew.** From that moment on, we *stayed* outside for the rest of the day.

Leading, Learning, and the Power of Prayer

In my early 30s, I was given another **leadership position** in my church—a responsibility I didn't take lightly. I am deeply grateful that my former pastor saw something in me and trusted me enough to bring me onto the **Board of Management as a Trustee.** What I didn't fully realize at the time was that he had **high expectations for me**—the same kind of expectations he had for his own children. Looking back, I know that at some point in my early 20s, I probably **let him down**. But that disappointment didn't come from a place of judgment—it came from **wanting more for me**. He wanted me to push beyond my comfort zone, to **strive for more**, to recognize that I was capable of **greatness in every area of my life**. Both he and **my Uncle David** held me to a **higher standard**, and for that, I will always be grateful.

Praying for Your Children Is Not Enough

As believers in Jesus Christ, staying on our **knees in prayer for our children** is necessary—but it's *not enough*. Even as they grow into adults, **they will still make mistakes**—sometimes, even bigger ones than we ever did. And while prayer is *essential*, it must be followed by **action**. **Prayer is a verb—it's an action word.** When we are on our knees, praying over our children and grandchildren, asking God to **protect them, guide their decisions, and shape them into contributors to society instead of menaces to society**, that is when our prayers become **activated**. But prayer alone isn't where our stewardship ends.

We must also be **good stewards** over **what God has given us**—not just **money**, but **wisdom, experience, and survival tools**. If we don't **pass down knowledge**, our children will be left **unprepared** for the battles ahead. Yes, they may **ignore our advice**, brush off our lessons, or **refuse to apply what we teach them right away**. But believe me—**they hear us**. And when they find themselves alone with their thoughts, alone with their struggles, and alone **before God**—that's when everything we poured into them will come rushing back. **They will remember. They will listen. And, in time, they will understand.**

Sidenote: Playing Church vs. Living It

When I was a little girl, I used to **play Church**—a lot. We would pretend the **Holy Spirit** had touched us. We would start shouting, dancing, falling out, and waving our hands like we had seen the adults do. It was all fun, an innocent imitation of what we thought faith looked like. As I grew older, **God allowed me to experience moments that would bring out those very same responses—for real.**

As a child, I was **sickly**.

As a teenager, I was **bullied**.

As a young adult, I was **assaulted**.

And when I became *grown, grown,* I was **diagnosed with breast cancer—twice**.

Through every season, every trial, and every tear, I learned something powerful: **We are never too old to learn. And we should never play Church.**

Know Your Worth & Stop Settling

I once saw a post on a Christian woman's social media page about relationships. She talked about how **when choosing a partner, you should know they want to be with you because you're** *special*, **not just because you're** *available*. The post had a tagline that hit me hard: "**Stop auctioning yourself off to the lowest bidder.**" Whew! **That took me back.**

I remember being younger, **chasing after the low-hanging fruit**, asking the guy out to dinner, making the plans, initiating the calls—just so I **wouldn't be alone**. That wasn't confidence. That wasn't power. **That was desperation. Whoo, chile!** *God has delivered me from that!*

Held to a Higher Standard

As we age and mature, **regardless of our role, we are held to a higher standard**—not because of our **gender, race, or background**, but simply because of **who we are**. Some people **expect excellence from me**, yet still try to engage me in **low-level activities** or push me to **lower my standards**.

The crazy thing? **The very same people who hold me to a high standard probably see more in me than I see in myself.** That might be **why** I feel **so much pressure**—like I'm constantly being *picked on*. It's a strange feeling when people see you as a **9 on a scale of 1 to 10**, but you don't even see yourself past a **4 or 5**. That disconnect doesn't happen overnight. **It's built over years—** through past **traumas**, hurtful **words spoken over us**, and wounds that never fully healed. Those things **shaped my self-esteem then**, and some of them still **affect how I see myself now**. Here's what I *do* know: **God sees the 10, a**nd every day, I'm working on seeing it too.

Signs, Distractions & Divine Moments

Have you ever prayed **out loud**—asking God for a sign—then looked up, to the left, to the right, or even down... and saw a **rainbow**? That's not a coincidence. Yes, the **enemy can hear your prayers** when you speak them aloud. But here's the thing—**the enemy cannot create rainbows.** Only **God** can do that. So when you receive that sign, **believe it, accept it, and move forward with confidence.**

Pay Attention—Distractions Can Cost You Everything

Get off your phone. Lift your head. Pay attention. I once knew a girl who **stepped off a curb** without looking up. She was busy staring at her phone. And in that moment, she **lost her life.**

Distractions **can** lead to destruction.

Distractions **can** lead to decimation.

Distractions **can** lead to *death.*

Not just a **physical** death, but the slow, silent death of **dreams, visions, and opportunities**— things that were meant for us but were lost because we weren't paying attention.

A Divine Reminder

I remember when I first moved to **Orange County** in California. One day, outside a grocery store, I heard a **young man singing** a worship song. I was drawn to him, so I walked over and started a conversation. He was collecting money for a trip, but what caught my attention wasn't the fundraiser—it was the **song.** It was familiar. Before I knew it, **I was singing harmony with him.** For a brief, beautiful moment, we worshiped together—a total **stranger and me, singing to the same God.** That wasn't random. That was **God reminding me He was there, too.**

Random Thoughts & Reflections

A Side Note on Fairness (or the Lack Thereof)

Ever thought about how **small-town politics** work? Imagine living in a town with a **tiny** police department—only **10 sworn officers**—yet there are **12 months in a year**. That means someone is getting *Officer of the Month* twice in one year. That's a flaw in the system that needs to be addressed.

A Mother's Sacrifice & Silent Struggles

My **mother worked hard**—too hard, really. Yet, despite her exhausting schedule, she still made time for us. She was there for our **band performances, choir recitals, dance showcases, football games, and basketball games** whenever she could. She worked **at least two jobs** as long as I've known her, doing whatever it took to give us a **better life**.

Looking back, I realize something else—**she was also running.** She wasn't just working hard to provide; she was **running from her past, her pain, and the grip of domestic violence.** She was running from **controlling men**—or maybe just **one particular man**. At the same time, she longed to be loved—and *loved well.*

A Mother's Instinct & My Silence

I believe all mothers—especially Black mothers— have that *gut feeling* when something is wrong with their child, or when someone has *wronged* their child. I don't think my mother **knew** I was being molested, but I believe she **suspected something**. And yet, she never asked. Maybe she was **too afraid of the answer**. I don't blame her. As I get older, I refuse to stay silent anymore. **I make noise.** Even so, I battle **my own insecurities**—the fear of unwanted attention, the anxiety of what might happen if I open my mouth. At this stage in my life, I am **pushing myself out of my comfort zone.**

111

I am **choosing to speak** because my **legacy** is bigger than me. It lives on in my **children, grandchildren, godchildren, community, friends, and their children**. Staying quiet about what is **right** is no longer an option. Being **this candid and vulnerable for the past 12 years has not been easy**, but I am doing my best to **shine a light—not necessarily on myself, but on others.** This book is **not about exposing anyone**. It's about showing **how they played a role in my life**, which is why their names have been changed or left out.

Seeing But Not Seeing

As the **youngest of nine**, I don't think I was **shielded from much**—I just didn't care to know what was happening around me **as long as it didn't interfere with my world**:

✓ My **playtime** outside

✓ My **snack time**

✓ My **nap time**

✓ My **church time**

✓ My **family time**

✓ My **friends from school**

I think my mother **indirectly** shielded me—or maybe she simply **kept things from me** because

I was the youngest, and I was a **girl**. That shaped how I see things even now. One day, I sent a text to a few close friends—**people I trusted to tell me the truth**. One of them responded with something that stopped me in my tracks:

"You seem oblivious to the things happening around you, and it makes you vulnerable." I never saw it that way. I thought I was **protecting myself**—choosing **not** to acknowledge what was **obvious** so I could have **plausible deniability**. That way, I could say, *"I don't know."* That way, I wouldn't have to **deal with the weight of the truth—even when it was staring me in the face**. I'll explore that further.

The Absence of a Father—Or So I Thought

Growing up in a single-parent household, I never really felt like I was missing out on being Daddy's little girl—because I had my pastor and my Uncle David.

I still had:

✓ Fishing trips

✓ Dances

✓ Lessons and guidance that many little girls get from their fathers

I didn't start feeling the absence of my father until I was around 14 or 15. By then, my needs had changed. I noticed that my pastor was pouring more into his own daughters because they were growing up. And my uncle? He was doing the same for his girls. Though both men still made time for me, they weren't my father—and that difference became clear. Uncle David always told us he felt like we were his kids. But in reality, he wasn't.

The Wild Child Who Loved to Play

As a kid, I was **all about the outdoors**. I played with my brothers, rode bikes, roller-skated, climbed fences, fought boys, played with marbles and jacks, and **sprinted across playgrounds in perfectly pressed dresses with matching ribbons in my hair**. By lunchtime? That neat and polished look was *gone*.

✓ Knees **scraped up from playing in the dirt**

✓ Hair **disheveled from fighting a boy who pulled my ponytail**

✓ Hands **covered in chalk from drawing on the pavement**

I made **friends easily**—probably because I was so active and social. But when **puberty hit**, my world shifted. I still **loved playing sports**, but I also started seeing things differently. I preferred playing against **boys** because, at the time, the girls didn't challenge me enough on the **basketball court** or the **football field**. Hanging around my **older brothers** made me tough. They told me, *"If you're gonna hang with us, you can't cry about every little thing."* So, I **rode my bike with them, roller-skated with them, climbed chain-link fences and brick walls just to keep up.** My **brother Vincent** was my **best friend** throughout my childhood and teenage years. That changed when he **left to college**. He found **new friends**—and I found a new best friend in my **cousin Dena.**

Lessons, Growth & Final Thoughts

One huge benefit of **having a lot of siblings**? You **always** have a **playmate.** We used to **raid the linen closet, tie towels around our necks, and pretend we were superheroes.** My mother **hated it**—because we **ruined** so many towels for no reason.

Spiritual Cancer & Church Hurt

Did you know many of us have **undiagnosed cancer**? Not the kind that shows up on a CT Scan—But the kind that **eats away at our souls:**

☑ Gossip

☑ Low self-esteem

☑ Jealousy

☑ Envy

☑ Bitterness

☑ Pride

We **are** the church. So whatever **happens inside us**, we take into the **physical** building. That's how **hurt spreads**. That's why **pettiness lingers**. That's why so many of us are stuck in **middle school mindsets**, repeating the same lessons until we finally *graduate* and grow up.

Final Reflections

1. Are you **inconveniencing others** because of **your lack of preparation** or bad behavior?
2. **If you survived the Covid-19 Pandemic, how are you preparing for your future?**
3. Are you an **active participant** in your own **healing & growth**?
4. Rich people get **roaches too**.
5. **A broken heart doesn't just get "over"— it must heal.**
6. *Not everyone will live, but everyone will die.*
7. *If you live long enough, someone else's prayer will become your prayer.*

Are You a House or a Home?

A **house** can be built in months. A **home** takes **a lifetime. Are you move-in ready, or do you need to be rebuilt, stripped down to the studs?**

Epilogue: A Final Reflection on S.E.X.

I've been in church since I was in my mother's womb. Much of what you've read in this book comes from **listening in on grown folks' conversations**, old and new sermons, and the life lessons I absorbed along the way. Here's one of the greatest things I've learned:

Introspection is Three-Fold:

1. **Looking within yourself with open eyes.**
2. **Allowing someone you trust to tell you what they see.**
3. **Asking God to reveal what He sees.**

Let's be real—it's not easy to let people **"tell you about yourself."** It's hard to admit that something **needs to change** or that some things **need to be left behind**. But growth *requires* honesty. And honesty *requires* humility.

Shifting Titles & Changing Labels

When I was a kid, we had **trash men**. Now, they're called **"Disposal Engineers."**

Housewives and stay-at-home moms were once seen as **traditional roles**, but society shifted, and the title "**stay-at-home mom**" became "**Domestic Engineer.**" Ironically, with the rise of reality TV, *Housewives* is back in style—even if some of them aren't married. We've changed **titles, labels, and terminology** to fit new narratives. I didn't hear the term **African American** until the **late '80s early '90s**—before that, we were simply called **Black people**.

✓ White people became **Caucasians**.

✓ People from South Korea, North Korea, the Philippines, Thailand, China, and Japan used to be called **Orientals**—now, they're part of the **Asian population**.

✓ The word **Mexican** has been used both culturally and as an insult, but now, the more inclusive phrase is "**Spanish-speaking communities**" or "**Latina" or "Latino.**"

These **changes were necessary**—they weren't just about being politically correct, but about **breaking stereotypes, dismantling negativity, and giving people the respect they deserve.**

Understanding S.E.X. Appeal—The Real Meaning

Each chapter in this book had a **subtitle that asked a question**—questions meant to **provoke thought** and **spark reflection**. Understanding **S.E.X. Appeal** means **knowing what you're made of**:

✓ **Your mind is the thinker.**
✓ **Your will is the chooser.**
✓ **Your emotions are the feelers.**

And since I said we'd talk about **S.E.X.**, let's talk about it.

Sex is a gift from God. It is meant to be shared **between a man and a woman within a marriage/covenant relationship**. Anything outside of that is not aligned with **God's design**. There. **Back to S.E.X.**

Tethered to the Wrong Things?

Do you remember the old **cartoon "CatDog"**? A cat and a dog conjoined at their rear ends—one body, two heads. It seemed funny back then. But now, looking back, I see something deeper—it was a **toxic relationship** in the worst way. Neither the **cat** nor the **dog** could separate. They had **no independence**. They had **no way to function properly**. They were **stuck together**, whether they liked it or not. So let me ask you—**what are you tethered to that is wrong?**

Confusion from **multiple sources** causes **scattered thoughts** and **wrongful behaviors**. Not knowing **who you are** or **what you contribute** leads to a **lack of direction**. And that leads to **one-night stands that turn into long days of lying to yourself and others.** You say you've **closed the door** on that toxic relationship, but **you're still peeking through the window.**

Smoke Breaks & Self-Reflection

Every time you take a **smoke break**, you are **dropping something off** and **picking something up. Pieces of you are scattered** because you don't want to stop and say: *"I am the problem."* I mentioned earlier that I've **only truly been using wisdom for the last 10 to 12 years.** That means for a long time, I **thought** I was doing well. I thought I was *wise,* but **growth is a process.** And part of that process is **forgiveness—of others and of yourself**. There is **someone you need to apologize to.** There is **someone I need to apologize to.** My prayer is that **God reveals it to me before I die.** If you're **genuine in your desire to grow**, He *will* reveal it to you, too. And when He does? **You must be obedient and follow through—no matter how difficult it is.**

Final Reflections: Are You the House or the Home?

It takes **nine to twelve months** to **build a house**. Building a home takes **a lifetime**. Some houses need **an extra room** added to accommodate growth. Some need **a complete foundation**

rebuild. Are **you** move-in ready? Or do you **need to be taken down to the studs and built up properly?**

Final Words: Get Right, Get Ready

My **past connections** and **old distractions** kept me from **focusing on my purpose**. These are called **historical hindrances**. All relationships have a **purpose**—but if you don't **identify the purpose**, that relationship can become **perverted and unhealthy**. Some people are **secretly competing** with you—your **spouse, friend, boss, children, even siblings**. You need to tell them: *"I'm already fighting the devil. I don't have time to fight you, too."*

Godly Relationships Over Toxic Ties

✓ **Ladies, you need a Ruth & Naomi soul tie—** one that is **pure, strong, and untainted by jealousy.**
✓ **Men, you need a Paul & Silas soul tie—** where **iron sharpens iron, and accountability is welcomed.**

Church hurt is **real**, and it cuts **deep**. At some point, you must **stop blaming the hurt and start healing from it.**

✓ "I was wrong."

✓ "It's my fault."

✓ "It's their fault."

✓ "I'm sorry."

✓ "I panicked."

✓ "I want to contribute to my healing and do better."

If you don't do this, the damage will only last **longer**.

Emotional Stress & Letting Go

✓ Raise your hand if you've **ever dealt with emotional stress.**

✓ Say *"I do"* if you know people who will **never achieve "relationship goals"**—not just the ones they post on social media, but the ones that *truly* matter.

Do you want **dysfunction** or **peace**? **God has better for you.** Once you get it **right with God**, you will get it **right within**, and **then** you will truly see. Let go of the **knuckleheads**—both male and female. Stop **catching feelings** for the wrong people.

Get Ready for What's Next

✓ **Search your agreements.**
✓ **Search your friendships.**
✓ **Search your partnerships.**

Be honest about **who you are** and **where you are**. It won't be easy, but **it is necessary**. **Pray. Seek wisdom. Move forward.** And remember this: **You can *NEVER* have too much S.E.X.**

About the Author

Laura A. Franklin is, first and foremost, a Christian woman—not perfect, but forgiven. She is the proud mother of five amazing adult children and the devoted grandmother of four extraordinary grandchildren. She also shares her heart and home with two beloved rescue dogs: 9ine, a spirited Terrier, and Smoke, a loyal Lab-Pit mix.

Deeply committed to her community, Laura has served as the only Housing Commissioner in her city for three years, advocating for inclusion, diversity in leadership, and equity for all.

She holds:

✓ An Associate of Arts degree in Liberal Studies

✓ An Associate of Science degree in Behavioral Studies

✓ **A Bachelor of Science degree in Human Services Management**

Additionally, she is a **Certified Professional Life Coach** and a **Certified Cognitive Behavioral Life Coach**, equipping her to guide individuals toward personal and spiritual growth.

Professional Training & Advocacy

Laura has received **chaplaincy training** from the **University of Maryland**, preparing her to assist in:

✓ **Death notifications**

✓ **Suicide prevention**

✓ **Domestic violence advocacy**

She has also trained with the **Southern Baptist Association of Southern California**, specializing in:

✓ **Disaster relief assistance**

✓ **Disaster cleanup**

✓ **Disaster recovery efforts**

Her **passions** include **education, mentoring youth and young adults, volunteering in women's ministry leadership groups, mental health awareness, and developing effective tools to assist children on the Autism Spectrum**.

Published Works

Laura is the author of several books, including:

⬜ **The Preacher and the Princess** *(2015)*

⬜ **I Stuff My Bra...So What? "A Beauty for Ashes Cancer Journey"** *(2020)*

⬜ **Richard A. Reid: The Man, The Music, and His Ministry – The Journey of a Living Legend** *(2022)*

Beyond her own publications, Laura has also worked as a **ghostwriter** across multiple genres, bringing other authors' stories to life.

Music & Songwriting

In **2004**, Laura penned her first song, ***"You Can Use Me"***, which is featured in her book *I Stuff My Bra...So What?* The song holds an official **Copyright with the Library of Congress**.

Other songs in her catalog include:

🎵 **"Please Come Home"**

🎵 **"Welcome"**

Each of these songs has been played and performed at **her home church**, further cementing her passion for **faith, worship, and storytelling**.

Laura A. Franklin is a woman of **faith, strength, and purpose**—committed to **empowering others, advocating for her community, and using her voice to inspire lasting change**.

A 21-Day Devotional:

Self-EXamination and Growth

This devotional is meant to spark deep reflection and inspire action. Take time each day to pray, journal, and set goals based on your insights. Are you ready for transformation?

Day 1: Breaking Free from Old Beliefs

Scripture: *Romans 12:2 (NIV) – "Do not conform to the pattern of this world, but be transformed by the renewing of your mind. Then you will be able to test and approve what God's will is—his good, pleasing and perfect will."*

Reflection: What is one belief you've held about yourself for years that may no longer be true? How has this belief shaped your decisions? Is it time to let it go or redefine it? Write down one old belief and replace it with a new, God-affirming truth.

Day 2: Recognizing Recurring Challenges

Scripture: *Proverbs 26:11 (NIV) – "As a dog returns to its vomit, so fools repeat their folly."*

Reflection: What recurring challenge in your life keeps showing up? What role do you play in it? Is it a pattern caused by past experiences, fears, or habits you need to break? Identify a recurring challenge, pray for wisdom, and commit to making one change this week.

_____

_____

_____

_____

_____

_____

_____

_____

_____

Day 3: Meeting Your Past Self

Scripture: *Philippians 1:6 (NIV) – "Being confident of this, that he who began a good work in you will carry it on to completion until the day of Christ Jesus."*

Reflection: If the version of you from five years ago met you today, what would they admire most? What would they warn you about? List one area of growth and one area that still needs work. Set a goal to address the latter.

_____

_____

_____

_____

_____

_____

_____

_____

Day 4: Facing What You Avoid

Scripture: *2 Timothy 1:7 (NIV) – "For the Spirit God gave us does not make us timid, but gives us power, love and self-discipline."*

Reflection: What is something you've been avoiding that, if confronted, could free you emotionally or mentally? What's stopping you from facing it? Take one small step toward confronting this issue today.

_____

_____

_____

_____

_____

_____

_____

Day 5: Evaluating Your Relationships

Scripture: *1 Corinthians 15:33 (NIV) – "Do not be misled: 'Bad company corrupts good character.'"*

Reflection: Who in your life drains your energy, and who fuels it? Are you investing too much in relationships that deplete you instead of those that uplift you? Identify one energy-draining relationship and one life-giving relationship. Adjust your time and attention accordingly.

_____

_____

_____

_____

_____

_____

_____

_____

_____

Day 6: Overcoming Fear

Scripture: *Joshua 1:9 (NIV) – "Have I not commanded you? Be strong and courageous. Do not be afraid; do not be discouraged, for the Lord your God will be with you wherever you go."*

If fear wasn't a factor, what decision would you make today to change your life? Take one actionable step toward that decision today.

_____

_____

_____

_____

_____

_____

_____

_____

_____

_____

_____

Day 7: Learning Life's Lessons

Scripture: *James 1:5 (NIV) – "If any of you lacks wisdom, you should ask God, who gives generously to all without finding fault, and it will be given to you."*

Reflection: What is the biggest lesson life has been trying to teach you, and are you finally ready to learn it? Write down this lesson and create a plan to apply it moving forward.

_____

_____

_____

_____

_____

_____

_____

_____

Day 8: The Truth About You

Scripture: *"Then you will know the truth, and the truth will set you free." — John 8:32 (NIV)*

What is one belief you've held about yourself for years that may no longer be true? Has it shaped your choices in ways that no longer serve you? Ask God to reveal the truth about who you are today.

_____

_____

_____

_____

_____

_____

_____

_____

_____

Day 9: Facing the Unspoken

Scripture: *"Cast all your anxiety on Him because He cares for you." — 1 Peter 5:7 (NIV)*

What have you been avoiding that, if confronted, could bring freedom? Ask God for the courage to face it, even if just one small step at a time.

_____

_____

_____

_____

_____

_____

_____

_____

_____

_____

Day 10: Fearless Decisions

Scripture: *"For God has not given us a spirit of fear, but of power, love, and self-discipline."* — 2 Timothy 1:7 (NIV)

If fear wasn't a factor, what decision would you make today? What's stopping you? Step forward in faith, even if just a little.

Day 11: Lessons Waiting to Be Learned

Scripture: *"Teach us to number our days, that we may gain a heart of wisdom."* — Psalm 90:12 (NIV)

What lesson has life been trying to teach you? Are you finally ready to learn it? Pray for the wisdom to not just see the lesson but apply it.

_____

_____

_____

_____

_____

_____

_____

_____

_____

_____

Day 12: Knowing Your Worth

Scripture: *"I praise you because I am fearfully and wonderfully made."* — Psalm 139:14 (NIV)

Do you truly believe you are worthy of love, success, and happiness? If not, what is blocking you from embracing this truth?

_____

_____

_____

_____

_____

_____

_____

_____

_____

Day 13: Overcoming Regret

Scripture: *"There is now no condemnation for those who are in Christ Jesus."* — Romans 8:1 (NIV)

Is there a past mistake you're still holding onto? God's grace covers all. Release your regret and move forward.

_____

_____

_____

_____

_____

_____

_____

_____

_____

_____

Day 14: Your Internal Dialogue

Scripture: *"Let the words of my mouth and the meditation of my heart be acceptable in Your sight, O Lord."* — Psalm 19:14 (NIV)

What does your inner voice say about you? Is it kind or critical? Align your thoughts with God's truth about you.

_____

_____

_____

_____

_____

_____

_____

_____

_____

Day 15: Strength in Weakness

Scripture: *"My grace is sufficient for you, for my power is made perfect in weakness."* 2 Corinthians 12:9 (NIV)

Where do you feel weak? God's strength is enough. Rely on Him instead of your own abilities.

_____

_____

_____

_____

_____

_____

_____

_____

_____

Day 16: The Company You Keep

Scripture: *"Walk with the wise and become wise, for a companion of fools suffers harm."* — Proverbs 13:20 (NIV)

Do your closest relationships push you toward growth or hold you back? Pray for discernment in choosing your inner circle.

_____

_____

_____

_____

_____

_____

_____

_____

_____

Day 17: Redefining Success

Scripture: *"But seek first His kingdom and His righteousness, and all these things will be given to you as well."* — Matthew 6:33 (NIV)

What does success mean to you? Does your definition align with God's? Seek His direction.

_____

_____

_____

_____

_____

_____

_____

_____

_____

Day 18: Healing From Hurt

Scripture: *"The Lord is close to the brokenhearted and saves those who are crushed in spirit."* — Psalm 34:18 (NIV)

What hurt are you still carrying? Give it to God and allow Him to bring healing.

_____

_____

_____

_____

_____

_____

_____

_____

_____

Day 19: Facing the Mirror

Scripture: *"Examine yourselves to see whether you are in the faith; test yourselves."* — 2 Corinthians 13:5 (NIV)

When was the last time you examined your own character? What do you see? What needs refining?

Day 20: Taking Responsibility

Scripture: *"Each one should test their own actions. Then they can take pride in themselves alone."* — Galatians 6:4-5 (NIV)

What choices have led you to where you are? Take ownership of your path.

_____

_____

_____

_____

_____

_____

_____

_____

_____

Day 21: Dreaming Again

Scripture: *"For I know the plans I have for you, declares the Lord."* — Jeremiah 29:11 (NIV)

Have you stopped dreaming? Ask God to reignite your vision for the future.

_____

_____

_____

_____

_____

_____

_____

_____

_____

www.ingramcontent.com/pod-product-compliance
Lightning Source LLC
LaVergne TN
LVHW021454080426

835509LV00018B/2285